Conversations
with Scripture and
with Each Other

Conversations with Scripture and with Each Other

Spiritual Formation for Lay Leaders

M. THOMAS SHAW, SSJE

A COWLEY PUBLICATIONS BOOK

ROWMAN & LITTLEFIELD PUBLISHERS, INC.
Lanham • Boulder • New York • Toronto • Plymouth, UK

A COWLEY PUBLICATIONS BOOK
ROWMAN & LITTLEFIELD PUBLISHERS, INC.

Published in the United States of America
by Rowman & Littlefield Publishers, Inc.
A wholly owned subsidiary of The Rowman & Littlefield Publishing
Group, Inc.
4501 Forbes Boulevard, Suite 200, Lanham, Maryland 20706
www.rowmanlittlefield.com

Estover Road
Plymouth PL6 7PY
United Kingdom

British Library Cataloguing in Publication Information Available

Library of Congress Cataloging-in-Publication Data

Shaw, M. Thomas, 1945–
    Conversations with Scripture and with each other : spiritual formation
for lay leaders / M. Thomas Shaw.
        p. cm.
    ISBN-13: 978-0-7425-6279-0 (pbk. : alk. paper)
    ISBN-10: 0-7425-6279-4 (pbk. : alk. paper)
    1. Lay ministry—Episcopal Church. 2. Spiritual formation—Episcopal
Church. 3. Episcopal Church—Doctrines. 4. Church—Biblical teaching.
5. Bible. N.T. Gospels—Criticism, interpretation, etc. I. Title.
BX5968.S53 2008
283'.73—dc22   2007050916

Printed in the United States of America

™
∞ The paper used in this publication meets the minimum requirements of
American National Standard for Information Sciences—Permanence of
Paper for Printed Library Materials, ANSI/NISO Z39.48-1992.

In thanksgiving for my parents
Wilma Sylvia Jones Shaw
Morvil Thomas Shaw Jr.

Contents

Preface

I NEVER INTENDED to write a book about building Christian community. I wanted our diocese to grow in numbers simply through people being attracted by the richness of our life together. And so I read everything I could read about church growth. All my reading seemed to lead me back to the first century of the church's life. I visited Palestine and Israel in order to understand the context of Jesus' ministry. I visited Greece and Turkey to understand Paul better. And I sought out a New Testament scholar, who for several years not only directed my reading and answered my questions but also refuted many of my observations and assumptions about life in the early church.

She reminded me that there was no ordained leadership in the early church, just men and women whose lives had been profoundly changed through Jesus Christ. The more I studied, the more I realized how much time these men and women of the New Testament communities spent discussing their faith, particularly what form their life together in Christ should take, most especially their common worship.

In the end, I wrote this book to get people talking. The more I studied these New Testament communities, and the more I listened to the hopes and faith of contemporary lay leadership, the more convinced I became that just as God did with these early Christian churches, so also today God offers us a way forward in our life together, through conversation. Alongside my studies, I continued in my vocation as a bishop in the Episcopal Church, almost every week of the year visiting the parishes of the Diocese of Massachusetts and listening to people like you who are now reading this book.

They, too, wanted their parishes to grow. Listening to them in the context of my ongoing studies, I became convinced that church growth and other aspects of Christian living cannot flourish except as we engage in conversation with scriptures. How we talk about Jesus' death and resurrection and the Eucharistic meal we share each Sunday, what Paul thought about money, how Matthew and his community thought about time, Mark's teaching about mission and outreach—all of these subjects at root have to do with conversion, and thus they also have everything to do with the building up of our congregations.

I invite you to engage scripture in such a way with me and then, in turn, with your congregation that it becomes for us the living word for the strengthening of your congregation and for the well-being of the world.

This isn't a book you have to read from beginning to end. The Introduction and the first two chapters provide a background, which will help in your discussions of the later chapters. But you should feel free to read and discuss the chapters in any order you find relevant to the life of your church. I simply encourage you to talk to one another. What you say to each other, the stories you tell each other, the relationship with God that you share, what attracts you to Jesus, and what it is that repels you from him—that is the real purpose of this book.

Acknowledgments

I AM GRATEFUL in the writing of this book to the many Christian communities over the years that have been the revelation of Christ's risen presence for me. I am especially thankful for the community of my brothers, my sister, and my parents—to whom this book is dedicated; my brothers in Christ in the community of the Society of St. John the Evangelist; and the community of the Episcopal Diocese of Massachusetts. They have all shown me everything I know of God's generosity, forgiveness, and love.

This book couldn't have been written without my extraordinary teacher, friend, and colleague, the Rev. Dr. Ellen Aitken. She has patiently guided my reading, answered my questions, read and corrected these pages, and doggedly encouraged me in this project for the last seven years. Because of her careful scholarship and wise faith, she has opened the four Gospels and Paul to me in ways that have changed my life as a Christian man and my ministry as a bishop.

I expect everyone who writes a book needs a good listener and articulate observer. Mine was my brother Geoffrey Tristram, SSJE, whose patience and thoughtful remarks I appreciate beyond measure.

Through their questions and concerns, congregations all across the Episcopal Diocese of Massachusetts have helped in the writing of this book. I am most thankful to The Rev. Tom Barrington, Amy Hunter, and the lay leaders of All Saints, Chelmsford, Massachusetts, who shared their time to discuss these chapters with me.

My thanks to Alex Baumgarten, Maureen Shea, and Tom Hart of the Episcopal Church's Office of Government Relations, who provided me with the information for the chapter on Outreach. My colleague Tracy Sukraw, editor of the *Episcopal Times;* my brother Kevin Hackett, SSJE; my friend Mary Oliver; and editor Ulrike Guthrie were all essential to the final crafting of this manuscript.

Finally, I am grateful to the Gabriel-Deveau family, my neighbors during the writing of this book. They offered me the comic relief, good meals, and conversation so necessary to the creative process. Fred Gabriel-Deveau, professional journalist and "no baloney" Christian that he is, brought his gifts of clarity and directness to many of these chapters.

I list some books that have been especially helpful to me in my reflecting, praying, and writing, in hopes that you might also pick up one or the other of them:

Hearing the Whole Story, by Richard A. Horsley, Westminster John Knox, 2001.

The Gospel of Matthew in Current Study, edited by David E. Aune, Eerdmans, 2001.

Social-Science Commentary on the Synoptic Gospels, by Bruce J. Malina and Richard L. Rohrbaugh, Fortress Press, 1992.

The Interpretation of Matthew, edited by Graham Stanton, SPCK, 1983.

History, Culture, and Religion of the Hellenistic Age, by Helmut Koester, Walter de Gruyter, 1995.

The Gospel of Matthew, edited by Daniel J. Harrington, SJ, The Liturgical Press, 1991.

Resurrection Reconsidered, by Gregory J. Riley, Fortress Press, 1995.

Centuries of Holiness, by Richard Valantasis, Continuum, 2005.

The First Urban Christians, by Wayne A. Meeks, Yale University Press, 1983.

Remembering the Poor, by Dieter Georgi, Abingdon, 1965.

The Resurrection of the Son of God, by N. T. Wright, Fortress Press, 2003.

Introduction

THIS IS A BOOK about talking to one another. In the years that I have served as the Episcopal bishop of Massachusetts, since 1994, people in parishes have said a lot to me in countless meetings and conversations. Listening to them—to people like you—is one of the real gifts to me in this ministry. In these conversations, people are in turns passionate, vulnerable, confused, definite, loving, supportive, and sometimes confrontational and angry. But we keep talking. Talking to one another, sharing conversations with each other, has been critical to the Christian faith since the death and resurrection of our Lord Jesus Christ.

Let me share a conversation I had recently:

"What do you think happened?" I asked my New Testament tutor one afternoon, as we were studying the resurrection stories in the Gospels and the letters of Paul. She replied, as she often does, with another question: "What do you mean?" She is a very careful scholar, so I answered, "What do you think happened in those twenty or so years after the resurrection of Christ and before Paul wrote that first letter to the Christians in Thessalonica?"

She paused for a long time, and then she said, "I think it went something like this. I believe that these men and women who had been Jesus' disciples during his public ministry, and perhaps some of them his friends even before that, had never been so loved before by anyone and had never before had such a tangible experience of the kingdom of God. Each had a profound experience of the risen Christ. The fact that Christ was alive motivated them to go out to tell their story as they searched for meaning in this event. In gatherings over meals, as they discussed the Hebrew scripture with each other, those who had never met Jesus found him present in the meal and in the gathered community."

In other words, Christian community formed as people talked, listened, and ate together. Christian community came into being as people reflected on who this Jesus of Nazareth was for them and how he had affected their lives. As they talked about Jesus in their communities, they began to change the world. So, too, do our Christian communities take on shape as we reflect together on who Jesus Christ is for us today and how he changes our lives. Like our ancestors in the faith, the way we talk about Jesus, the way we have "conversations" with scripture and with each other, could change the world.

I hope that this book will get you to talk to one another. When you and others like you talk to me when I visit your churches, God's vision for our communities begins to emerge. Together, we continually try to find God's desire for the church. Conversation within the community strengthens the body of Christ—and changes the world.

The questions in this book are certainly for your individual prayer and reflection while reading. But they are also to stimulate group conversation in your vestry meeting, adult education class, or any lay leadership meeting in your church. Your own wisdom will direct you to those questions that seem appropriate or helpful to your community.

If, for example, your vestry or committee meets once a month, select a chapter for all of you to read in the month before your next meeting. After finishing the chapter, spend a little time reflecting on your church in light of what you have read. Then consider the questions or conversation prompts on that topic at the end of the chapter. Which of the questions are the most important for you? Does the material in the chapter raise questions or concerns of your own that you would like to discuss? At the beginning of the next meeting, after you've gathered yourselves with a prayer, spend just twenty minutes or so with the questions that seem most important to your committee. You don't necessarily need to come to any conclusions. My prayer and hope are that your discussion will inform the business of your committee over the months to come—and that you will keep the conversation going.

CHAPTER ONE

Conversations
about Community

WHAT ARE THE challenges you face in your congregation? If you are the treasurer, you might respond, "Pledging is up this year, but with rising health insurance costs, heating costs, and the unexpected roof repairs on the church, we are going to have another deficit budget this year." If you are the senior warden or elder, you might respond, "We are getting some new families, but it tends to be the same small group of us year after year who serve on the vestry, teach in the church school, run the Christmas fair, and attend diocesan events. We all have jobs and families; it's a lot for us to juggle."

So why do you do it? Why do you spend all of this time on budgets, buildings, and fund-raising? Typically, you say, "We do it for the community." You tell me it's where you've raised your children, the place where you were surrounded with support and love when you lost your job or when someone in the family was seriously ill. Sometimes you say that in times of overwhelming need in your life, you find the compassion of the risen Christ in each other. It's where you come week after week for the same sense of peace Christ gave to his disciples when he appeared to them in Jerusalem. This gift of peace gives you some perspective in a world that seems way too busy and often out of control. Or you tell me that the community of the church kept your marriage together, or that when your marriage failed, church was the only place you experienced forgiveness.

You tell me you felt lost when you emigrated from Nigeria, until you found the familiarity of the Anglican tradition in your local Episcopal church. Or that it was the place you first experienced acceptance when you came out as a lesbian. Or that church was the place where you could honestly talk to others when you faced your addiction. You tell me that as a teenager in leadership, your church community is the one place you can be yourself and where you don't experience peer pressure or teachers with excessive expectations.

You tell me that unlike your work environment or your extended family or friendship circle, the church community is the only place where you can talk about your spiritual life and how much it means to you. You say that when you came from the Dominican Republic as a single mother, the church community cared about you enough to provide an after-school program for your kids and an English as a Second Language course so you could get a job. It is the place, you tell me, through which you are motivated to join God in alleviating suffering in the world. It is through your life in the church community that the face of God is revealed to you, you say.

When you talk like this, I hear the echo of Paul's words to the Corinthian church: "Now you are the body of Christ and individually members of it" (I Corinthians 12:27). For when you speak of how much you value the community of your church, it is clear that the building that houses the community is not most critical to you. Instead, it is the people who gather in the buildings for worship each week and how you relate to one another as followers of Jesus Christ that is of primary value to you. It's the fellowship, what you learn from one another about God, and how you experience God's grace through one another that matters so much to you. You often say your relationship with God actually depends on the people who gather to share the Eucharist, the risen presence of Christ in the bread and wine of communion. It is this belief in God that is the common denominator.

Talking about What Community Means for Your Church

Pause for a few moments now and think about why you are particularly grateful for the community of the church. Reflect on how it is through this community that you are desiring and coming to a deeper relationship with God. Talk to each other about how that relationship or desire couldn't have grown the way it has if it weren't for these people with whom you pray every week, with whom you drink coffee after the service, with whom you attend meetings and work on projects for the building up of the church.

Is all the time, effort, and frustration that goes into sustaining your congregation worth it to you? Why? What do you wish could be changed in your life together? Where do you turn when you're feeling ambivalent about whether it's all worth it? Probably most of us at some time think it'd be easier to go it alone and not have to depend on others who are so different.

Letting Scripture Talk

Community is at the heart of the New Testament Church. The love and necessity of community for the living out of our Christian witness that are expressed by the vestries I listen to Sunday after Sunday are deeply rooted in the faith of our ancestors. The oldest piece of literature we have in the New Testament, Paul's first letter to the Thessalonians, written most likely just twenty years after the death and resurrection of our Lord Jesus Christ, is written not to an individual, but to a small, struggling, courageous community on the coast of the Mediterranean, in what is now Greece. In this very first letter of the New Testament, Paul commends his brothers and sisters in Christ for the way they, as a community of faith, have received the gospel of Jesus Christ and for how they, as a community, have been a model for believers throughout their whole region. In this earliest of letters, Paul is already telling his readers how to build up their community: "Be at peace among yourselves. And we urge you, beloved, to admonish the idlers, encourage the fainthearted, help the weak, be patient with all of them. See that none of you repays evil for evil, but always seek to do good to one another and to all. Rejoice always, pray without ceasing, give thanks in all circumstances; for this is the will of God in Christ Jesus for you" (I Thessalonians 5:13–18).

The building up of community is seen as a primary vocation for the leadership of the Christian community from the very beginning. In fact, with the exception of the letter to Philemon, all of the letters of Paul and the Gospels of Matthew, Mark, Luke, and John were written not to individuals, but to communities. The authors of the Gospels and Paul could not have conceived of a relationship with God outside of the context of a community.

Unlike us, our first-century Mediterranean ancestors in the faith would have had very little sense of self or of individual fulfillment or achievement outside of the context of their family, household, clan, neighborhood, or ethnic identity. This was true for men and women, whether they were slaves, free members of society, or citizens of Rome. What an individual wanted for him- or herself was not nearly as important as what was necessary for the good of the family or the larger community.

Paul and the authors of Matthew, Mark, Luke, and John were people of their time, and they would not have known how to preach the gospel and experience the risen Christ except through the fellowship of others. But, community wasn't important to them only because it conformed to the contemporary pattern of life. As these early followers of Jesus Christ gathered together to talk, share a meal, pray, and read scripture, they were coming into deeper union with God through the suffering, death, and resurrection of Jesus Christ. Their time together transformed them all. Whether that transformation was fast or slow, the community shaped them—and shapes us— more and more into the image and likeness of God.

And so it is of little surprise to me that you give your time and energy to the demanding work of church leadership for the sake of the community.

But let's be truthful. As much as you care about your congregation, you also remind me that forming and nurturing a congregation are often hard and depleting work. Balancing budgets, maintaining property, resolving personnel issues, and tending to the inevitable conflict of parish life can seem far removed from the unfolding of the kingdom of God and the spiritual renewal we desire and cherish. I remember one meeting with a vestry, after a long summer of dealing with an expensive and complicated sewer project, when the rector remarked, "There has to be more to our life together in leadership than this. Sometimes when we are caught up in a project like this, we lose sight of why we are doing any of it in the first place."

Not long ago I visited a vestry during the time its parish was searching for a new rector. It had been a demanding year and a half for them. Not only were they without ordained leadership, but they also were amidst unexpected and expensive building renovations, negotiations with a child care center using the property, the sale of a valuable piece of real estate, and division in the parish over worship decisions made by the former rector. This interim period had required an unprecedented commitment on the part of every member of the vestry. They were tired, and there was some tension in the room between them as they told the story of their journey over the past months.

Because the work of the rector search committee was so important to the life of the parish, that group joined the vestry on the night we met together. When their turn came, the search committee members told a very different tale. While these men and women had made a time commitment equal to that of the vestry members, they were energized and hopeful about the future of the parish, and they were enjoying the company of one another while doing this demanding work of choosing a new rector. They described how they regularly prayed together and shared their spiritual journeys and the dreams they had for the future of their community, under new leadership. While they did not agree on every aspect of their life together, talking together about their faith had unified them.

When the search committee members finished with their story, there was a poignant silence, which was broken when one of the vestry members quietly commented, "I'm envious of what you on the search committee have experienced with one another."

Conversation with one another about God and their shared experience of Jesus Christ had given the members of the search committee the trust and unity they needed in order to fulfill their responsibility of choosing the ordained leadership necessary to the life of their congregation. Talking with one another about God had helped them discern a vision of what God might be calling their community to become in the future, with their new rector. But perhaps even more important than that, their conversations had renewed and deepened their faith. No wonder the vestry member was envious. Aren't we all searching for a deeper relationship with God?

Is this your experience? As a leader in the church, you know that balancing budgets, enlisting Sunday school teachers, and managing church property are tasks God has called you to do that are an integral part of your community. But are you envious of church groups who find spiritual renewal and purpose in their work? Do you feel almost defeated by how few resources you have at your disposal to do your work and by how little talent you actually have to do the task? Do you ever feel like the senior warden whose faith diminished during her tenure because of the demands of her responsibilities? In spite of your deep commitment to the community of the church, do you sometimes resent the many hours you spend at meetings, away from your work, your family, or deprived of the time you desperately need to relax? Do you long for the kind of encouragement Paul recommends to the church in Thessalonica? Do you long for that depth of prayer life that, Paul writes, makes it possible to give thanks in all circumstances?

Let us recapture why the community of faith is so important to us.

CHAPTER TWO

Listening to Paul and the Gospel Writers Speak to Their Communities

THE GOSPELS and the Epistles chosen were originally intended to build up the faith life of very particular communities professing a belief in Jesus Christ. They were not first and foremost intended for the edification and inspiration of individuals. While all these communities were dedicated to Jesus, like our own, each faced particular conflicts having to do with theology, money, worship, leadership, or gender, among a host of other issues. The early church leaders knew well the specific communities to which they were writing and had personally experienced the risen Christ in the context of community life. Accordingly, they arranged and told the narrative of Jesus' passion, death, and resurrection; the healing miracles; the parables; and the teaching of Jesus in specific ways. Their Gospels and Epistles became powerful sources of discernment and renewal for the leaders of the church communities to which they were addressed.

Listening to what they have to say inspires, informs, and invigorates us as leaders in the church today. How was Christ present to their communities? How were they being called to spiritual growth and mission?

Letting Scripture Talk: Paul's Communities

In the center of the Corinthian marketplace in Greece, a small sign attached to some stones states that from this very spot Paul had preached the gospel of Jesus Christ in Corinth. We can't be certain that Paul actually preached at that exact location, but we know from his letters and from the Book of Acts that he participated in the founding of the church in Corinth and ministered there for a considerable period of time. Certainly, I thought to myself as I stood there in the ruins, Paul walked through this marketplace, shopped here, listened to the public debates, talked with friends, and met visitors from all across the vast Roman Empire.

Corinth in the first century was a sprawling, thriving urban center, culturally and religiously diverse, with an active seaport, and at the crossroads of important trade routes. The ruins of the old port where Paul arrived in Corinth for the first time by boat are still there, just a short distance from the city. The same shops peopled by Paul's friends Priscilla and Aquila, though now abandoned like the rest of the city, line the marketplace and testify to the former prosperity of Corinth.

Standing there myself in the center of the marketplace on that warm summer morning, in brilliant sunshine, I began to get a sense of what Paul was up against. He would have seen the Temple of Apollo, with its statue of the god inside and its altar of sacrifice outside. As I stood there, I remembered how all along the road on the drive from Athens to Corinth earlier in the morning, I had seen small niches in the rocks where the people of Paul's time left offerings before little statues of the goddess of love, Aphrodite. Just a few minutes before, I had passed through a museum full of representations of various parts of the human anatomy, fashioned from clay, that would have been offered to Asklepius, the god of healing. Then my thoughts went back to the previous day. In Athens, on the Acropolis, I had seen the splendid statue of the goddess of wisdom. Statues of gods were everywhere, reminding me of the deep religiosity of the people of first-century Greece.

The Roman Empire was deeply religious, too. Because of the real possibility of natural disasters, such as plagues, fire, famine, and earthquakes, as well as human threats, such as slave revolts, everyone, from the emperor in Rome to the poorest slave, sought the protection of gods, and everything, from elaborate cultic oracles to arrangements of scattered dried chicken bones, was consulted concerning the fates of individuals, families, communities, or entire countries. Wherever Paul went on his missionary journeys, be it Philippi, Thessalonica, Ephesus, or anywhere else in the Mediterranean area, he had plenty of competition from the numerous religions of the day—the official religion of the state, mystery cults, and devotion to local gods and goddesses, whose origins were unknown and layered with myth and superstition. Yet Paul also knew this was fertile ground for a new religion like Christianity.

Partly because of the extensive Roman road system and seaports, partly because of the cultural and religious diversity of the large cities, and partly because the Jewish Diaspora tended to congregate in places like Rome, Ephesus, Antioch, and Corinth, most of Paul's missionary work seems to have been in these large urban areas. Because of the Jewish heritage of his ministry and preaching, Paul might enter a city like Corinth, find the local Jewish synagogue, and begin to tell its members of Jesus Christ. He seems to have had only partial success with his Jewish brothers and sisters, and so he also preached the gospel in the public marketplace and in the private homes of Gentiles.

From these public and private efforts in cities, small house churches formed. It was these communities that Paul visited and revisited, to which he wrote letters, and which he coached from the time of his conversion to Christianity until his death. Most likely, a city like Rome or Corinth would have had several of these little house churches, sometimes only nominally connected to one another. The makeup of the congregations would have been as diverse as their city. Unlike in most other religions of the first century, there were no initiation fees for membership in these small house churches, and so they were open to the poorest of the poor as well as to the wealthy. Women, it seems, played a more important leadership role in these house churches than they did in the larger society.

The people named in Paul's letters seem to indicate that the members of the churches came from all kinds of religious and ethnic backgrounds. Paul lived among and worked with them. It is clear from his letters that he knew them well. His visits to cities like Corinth or Philippi were often long, so he came to know the uniqueness of each church community and the values that were important to its city or country.

Talking about What Your Church Can Learn from Paul's Communities

In order to imagine that kind of diversity among twenty-five or thirty people, consider your own church and the different religious backgrounds represented in it. Reflect on the class, age, and gender differences, and what freedom in Christ might mean for these different members of your church community. As far as you know others' backgrounds or can imagine them, think how everyone has come to your church with their own ideas of how a religious community should be formed and what they liked or didn't like about their previous life of worship. Think of the different expectations the members have. Now imagine the same about the Corinthian church. And then think of all the sorting out that would have had to be done about rules, leadership, and worship. That is just a taste of the kind of Christian communities Paul was writing to from around 50 CE to 70 CE.

In the Episcopal Church, more than half of our membership comes from other Christian denominations and other faith communities, or has no religious background at all. As a leader in your church, how do you learn about and incorporate what these new Episcopalians offer us from their former religious experience? How do you invite their contribution to enrich the life of your community? As a leader in your church, what do you think is important for these new members to know about the Episcopal Church?

How are you exposing these new Episcopalians to the richness of your parish community and the communities of your local diocese, the national Episcopal Church, and the worldwide Anglican Communion?

Letting Scripture Talk: Mark's Communities

"Tell us about your life," one of the teenagers requests in halting Spanish as the six or seven of us stand in a circle in the tiny room with a dirt floor and no electricity. Our hostess is a young Honduran woman with five small children, living in a shack on the edge of a huge garbage dump outside the city of Tegucigalpa. Altogether, there are about thirty of us, mostly teenagers and a few adults, on a week-long mission to paint and landscape the little church of which this woman is a member. Every morning, when we arrive at the church, some of us begin painting or hauling dirt, while a smaller group of us makes pastoral calls on the parishioners of this new congregation, founded to care for the people who live near the garbage dump. Upon being invited into a home, one of the teenagers in our group asks the mother or the father of the household to tell us about their lives, their hopes for their children, the struggles they are facing, and what their church means to them. When we are done with our questions, we all join hands, and one of the teenagers leads us in prayer for the household.

This woman's story is heartbreaking. Because there was no work and no way to feed her children in the countryside, she has moved here from her village with her partner, the father of two of her children, himself not much older than these teenage boys standing now in her house. They hoped by moving here that he might get work in the city and she might be able to scavenge from the dump and sell what she finds. But despair has gotten to her partner; he drinks a lot, and when he is home, he beats her and sometimes the children, too. The little church by the river that we are helping to paint is the only place for her to go to for help; it is the only community for this mother and her children.

Her story isn't very different from that of hundreds of her neighbors living near this dump. They are all people forced off the land, and away from their families and networks of extended family care, and into these shantytowns because of the grinding poverty that has resulted from government corruption and worker exploitation by foreign companies. In fact, the stories of these people living near the garbage dump aren't very different from the stories of

countless people throughout human history who, because of powerful oppressors, wars, and natural disasters, have flocked to cities with
narrow alleys and crowded rooms, and into lives of hopeless poverty.

Among history's many such displaced people were those of the
Galilee and Jerusalem. For in the late 60s or early 70s, the time most
scholars believe the first of our Gospels, Mark, was written, the people
of Palestine were experiencing the full brunt of the Roman occupation. Because of triple taxation—from Rome, the puppet gover-
nors of the Roman Empire in Palestine, and the religious leadership
of the Temple—small farmers and villagers from the northern
Galilee were forced to give up their land. With the destruction of
the Temple in 70 CE and the upheaval caused by the war between
the Roman government and the Jewish people, Jews and Gentiles
alike fled Jerusalem and villages and towns for their own safety.

For many of these displaced people, the trading crossroad of
Antioch, a big, thriving city by first-century standards on what is now
the south coast of Turkey, became their destination and their hope of
a safer place in which to begin a new life and make a living. Some
of them were Christians from a Jewish background, others were
Christians from a Gentile background, and perhaps, travel being as
free as it was in those days of the empire, some of these in Antioch
were from as far away as Rome. Having landed in Antioch, these followers of Jesus of Nazareth and their traditions were now being
exposed to each other. It is for these communities, each with a different experience of the risen Christ, that Mark writes his Gospel.

Because of the upheaval of the times, these were not the more
religiously homogeneous communities for which Matthew's or
John's Gospels were written. Most likely, Mark found one group of
Christians in Antioch particularly devoted to Jesus the healer in the
tradition of a first-century wonder-worker. Another group of Christians there, it seems, was much more influenced by an experience of
Jesus as a powerful apocalyptic preacher. Yet another community's
life seems to have been centered on Jesus' parables and his teaching.
There was also a community that was particularly devoted to Jesus'
suffering on the cross. The prominence of John the Baptist in Mark's
Gospel leads many scholars to believe that there were also followers

of John the Baptist in Antioch, perhaps on the fringe of some of these communities, for whom Mark also wanted to find a place in the forming Christian Church.

So Mark wrote a Gospel in which he doesn't seem to judge the experience of one community as better than another. Unlike in the Gospel of John, you don't get the sense that anyone is to be excluded from the community of believers just because their experience or tradition of the risen Christ is different. Instead, Mark tried to unify the community around the suffering and crucifixion of Jesus, which we'll look at in more detail in chapter 3.

Talking about What Your Church Can Learn from Mark's Communities

I wonder what it might have been like for members of one of these little Jewish Christian or Gentile Christian cells in Antioch, having come from Syria, some part of the Galilee, or Jerusalem. Say it was a little displaced group from the northern Galilee whose faith in Jesus had been largely nurtured by his parables, handed down orally in its community for maybe thirty years. Perhaps these were the faith descendants of that first group that gathered around a meal to hear the witness of one of Jesus' followers who especially remembered Jesus' teaching and experienced his resurrection.

What was it like for them to hear for the first time of a very different tradition, of Jesus the healer or of Jesus the apocalyptic preacher? Would they have been excited by this new knowledge? Would they have seen it as an invitation from God for their community to expand and go deeper in its faith in Jesus? Or would they have been threatened by this new knowledge, fearful of some of the implications for their own tradition or the life of their small community? Would they have welcomed with gratitude Mark's efforts through his Gospel to bring unity to these different churches in Antioch?

As a leader, what different understandings of Jesus can you identify among the members of your church? What do the people you worship with every Sunday believe about Jesus Christ? What aspect of his risen presence is most important to them? Do they most value Jesus the moral teacher, Jesus the healer, Jesus the prophet, or Jesus the defender of the outcast? Often their hymn preferences will be an indication of their theology or theological world.

As a leader, how do you encourage people with these different experiences of Jesus to listen to and engage with one another as a way of providing spiritual growth and deeper conversion for the whole community?

Letting Scripture Talk: Matthew's Communities

In the early 1990s, I was part of a group staying in a convent in Nazareth. It was a warm, sunny fall day, and we were scheduled to have a quiet day, with a series of meditations by our chaplain in the convent chapel. I could not bear the thought of being cooped up in a chapel on such a beautiful day, and as much as I respected the chaplain, I could not imagine that he would have anything to say that would significantly enhance my relationship with God when I was in this particular frame of mind.

I knew that the first-century city of Sepphoris, with its beautiful mosaics, Roman villa, theater, and Jewish quarter, was just six kilometers away. While it is now a ruin, in the time of Jesus, Sepphoris was a thriving city with plenty of building going on. It's not inconceivable that if Joseph was a carpenter and Jesus followed him in his trade, the two of them walked together and worked in Sepphoris. Instead of retreating to the chapel, I decided to spend the day walking to Sepphoris and exploring this ancient city.

Once I got away from crowded Nazareth, the walk was lovely, and Sepphoris was everything the guidebooks said it would be. It being a weekday and outside of the tourist season, I had the whole site to myself for the entire day. At that time archeologists were just beginning to uncover the mosaics in the public buildings and on the main street of Sepphoris. The private villa on the hill overlooking the town, with its elaborate dining room and mosaics, was restored and exquisite, but what really captured my attention was the Jewish quarter. These were more humble dwellings than houses of the

Roman occupiers: whole families lived in one or two rooms, and the houses were crowded together along narrow alleyways. Even if it hadn't been labeled as the Jewish quarter, I think I would have known it, because every so often I would stumble across a mikvah, a plastered cistern used for Jewish ritual bathing, at the bottom of a few steps.

With the destruction of the Temple in Jerusalem in 70 CE, Judaism had lost its heart. Soon after, in this Jewish quarter in Sepphoris, a school developed under a great teacher who was dedicated to the study of Torah. There were many such schools founded in the last part of the first century to study Torah, or the Law. These learned Jewish men, perhaps Pharisees or scribes, believed that the Torah would be the new Temple of the Jewish faith, one that could never be destroyed and that the Jewish community could take with it no matter where it was displaced in the world. Even in foreign countries with governments that were hostile to Judaism, the Law would continue to form the people in their faithfulness to the one God and preserve their identity as a people.

It was for a community with a scribe and Pharisee tradition, like this Jewish quarter in Sepphoris, that the Gospel of Matthew was written some time late in the first century in western Syria, on the far side of the Sea of Galilee. This Christian community most likely grew from Jews dedicated to the Torah who, in their study of the Hebrew scripture, their listening to the stories of Jesus of Nazareth, and their experiencing his presence at the meal and in discussions, came to believe that Jesus was the Messiah, for whom the Jewish people had longed for centuries. The author of Matthew's Gospel did what these Jews dedicated to the Torah were doing, except he did it through the lens of Jesus of Nazareth. This is one of the reasons why Hebrew scripture is quoted so often in Matthew's Gospel, and why the Law and Jewish customs are referred to again and again in it. "Do not think," says the Jesus of Matthew's Gospel, "that I have come to abolish the law or the prophets; I have come not to abolish but to fulfill" (Matthew 5:17).

This was a violent and chaotic time for the Jewish people. Because of the war with the Roman government, not only was the

Temple destroyed, but whole villages had been burned. It was just the same for the Jewish Christians and maybe some Gentile Christians who were part of the community to whom Matthew wrote his Gospel. Violence is deeply engrained in the worldview of Matthew. By the telling of his Gospel story, he was trying to create and build community in this violent time. He wanted to give the people God had entrusted to him a kind of Law, or Torah, through the person of Jesus of Nazareth so they would be able to live within that violent world in a community that protects and upholds them.

Matthew might have been a Christian teacher, like one of the Jewish teachers of the Torah, who had a group of students gathered around him. At least this is the role in which he portrays Jesus in his Gospel. For example, Jesus asked his disciples, "Have you understood all this?" They answered, "Yes." And he said to them, "Therefore every scribe who has been trained for the kingdom of heaven is like the master of a household who brings out of his treasure what is new and what is old" (Matthew 13: 51 & 52). He might have been writing this Gospel for them as a kind of practical guide for forming Christian community as they went out to tell the story of Jesus Christ. It looks as though he wrote from his Jewish scribe tradition, and that he had a version of an already written Gospel of Mark, some writing that the author of Luke had as well, now lost to us, and stories he had heard quite independently of Mark, Luke, John, or Paul. From all of this material, as he prayed over it and reflected on the situation of his community and how he wanted to equip his students to do the work of God, he formed his Gospel.

Talking about What Your Church Can Learn from Matthew's Communities

In many ways, Matthew's is the most pastoral of the Gospels. A shrewd observer, Matthew obviously was quite familiar with the difficulties of living in Christian community. He knew how important are order, rules, and leadership for a group of people wanting to live together as brothers and sisters in Christ. For example, he knew that if people of different ages and backgrounds are going to live together in community, there frequently will be disputes, hurt feelings, and offense, so he remembered a story to tell from Jesus about forgiveness, the one in which Peter asks, "Lord, if another member of the church sins against me, how often should I forgive?" In effect, Jesus responds that Peter should forgive an infinite number of times (Matthew 18:21–23).

Vestry members frequently speak of receiving telephone calls or e-mails from parishioners who have been offended or angered by the rector or some decision in the church. I wonder: As a church leader, have you ever spoken in such circumstance of the need—indeed command—to forgive? Or do you more often play the middle person or try to placate the individual? What is hardest for you about living in the community of a parish? What are some of the issues of living together in a parish family that frequently surface? In what areas of communal life could you use some practical or spiritual guidance? Given what you know of Matthew's understanding of the importance of forgiveness for those living together in a church, how in your leadership do you draw on the Gospel of Matthew to help you guide your community? What is there that could help you?

Letting Scripture Talk: John's Communities

Rising dramatically above the northern edge of the Sea of Galilee is the Golan Heights. Before the 1967 war, this area belonged to Syria. Under the occupation of the Golan Heights by Israel, some of the land is now a nature preserve. The terrain in this nature preserve is rocky, and there are few trees. The views can be magnificent. There are deep canyons, waterfalls, and it is not uncommon to see eagles and vultures soaring above the cliffs. But there is nothing soft or appealing about this land.

My first visit to the Golan Heights took me to an archeological site of a synagogue ruin in a place called Gamala. This synagogue, many archeologists believe, is the oldest in the world. What remains of the village is on a hill that rises up from the floor of the canyon. It was a cold, rainy, windy November day when I visited. That treacherous walk down to the site, over slick black rock, made it easy to understand how the Jews had held out with such tenacity in a place like this after Rome had destroyed the Temple in Jerusalem. The place was practically impregnable.

With the destruction of the Temple in 70 CE, the center of Jewish life had been destroyed, and many Jerusalem Jews fled their city and established communities all over the Mediterranean region. With the Temple gone, these Jews were searching for a new heart. Some turned to Torah, or the Law, as the means of understanding God. Others turned to the more mystical side of Judaism, which was rich in images, themes of light and darkness, and heavenly visions. They also embraced the wisdom literature of their Hebrew scripture as a profound way of relating to God.

The Gospel of John was probably not written for the people of Gamala on the Golan Heights, where I was on that cold November morning. More likely, it was written for the small Christian communities a little north of Gamala. The communities of John were probably made up of Jews drawn more to the mystical and wisdom strands of Judaism than to Torah, or Law. When these Jews began to hear the stories about Jesus of Nazareth and his teachings, and as they came to believe he was indeed the Messiah, they were naturally drawn to a more mystical and divine understanding of him.

Because we are pretty certain that the Gospel of John was written late in the first century and maybe into the second century, it looks like the men and women of the communities of John had had plenty of opportunity to discuss and interpret everything they had heard about Jesus. They had had time to filter these stories and teachings of Jesus through their particular mystical and wisdom understanding of a faith life with God.

The Gospel of John probably wasn't written by just one person at one particular time, as were, say, the letters of Paul. Rather, there was an initial author of John, and then a decade or two later and then maybe a decade after that, other members of these communities of John came along and refined or tempered some of the original writing. John is a more layered Gospel than the other three Gospels.

Sometimes when I am reading certain chapters of the Gospel of John, a picture of an adult forum in one of our parishes comes to mind, not the kind of adult forum where someone who is knowledgeable about a particular subject gets up and speaks for forty-five minutes, and then the people present have a chance to ask questions; but one where someone just briefly outlines an issue in the church, and then everyone, from their understanding of God and their experience of the community of the church, offers an opinion or has the opportunity to question the opinion of someone else. The kind of forum where Christian men and women are trying to find truth together and understand that each person present, because they all abide in God, has some truth to offer is what comes to mind. This is the kind of forum where a high value is placed on mutuality and exchange.

Some of the passages in John, like the story of the blind man who receives his sight from Jesus, are like such a forum. The leader throws out a situation to the gathered fellowship: a man who is blind from birth. Then there are all the questions: Who sinned, the man or his parents? How are his eyes opened? Where is Jesus? What do you say about Jesus? How can a man who is a sinner perform such signs? Out come questions, reasons, and opinions from all different sides of the community until, at the end of all the discussion, it can be said, "If this man were not from God, he could do nothing" (John 9:33). It is a final statement about who the sisterhood and brotherhood to whom John is writing think Jesus is.

There are other passages like this in John: about the raising of Lazarus, about the Samaritan woman at the well, and about Thomas's meeting with the risen Christ, to name just a few. You get a sense of this fellowship being one where there was a high degree of trust, where the members loved each other and were committed to being with one another because they knew that it was in this group of people that they found Christ, and probably because they had little need for a well-defined hierarchical kind of leadership. The members of John's community seem to have been committed to dwelling with each other, loving one another, and together discovering the presence of Christ in their midst.

Perhaps this description also explains some of the difficult realities of John's community. In such an intimate fellowship with such a high degree of commitment, there was bound to be some judgment about those who had chosen to leave the common life in Christ or those who had chosen not to believe in God through Jesus Christ. There was obviously some real conflict surrounding this community that probably encouraged it to define very clear boundaries about who was a member and who was not a member. For example, because this church had been around for a while, the members had maybe as many as two or three generations to talk and pray about their experience of Jesus. It seems they became clearer and clearer about who Christ was for them. Therefore, the members of John's community may have become more and more the outsiders in the traditional Jewish community, which at one time at least tolerated their belief in Jesus as the Christ. It may have been that as the members in this fellowship of John became clearer about Christ, some of them were asked to leave the Jewish synagogue or left of their own accord. John's was a community that often made sharp distinctions and held strong opinions about those who were not part of its life.

Talking about What Your Church Can Learn from John's Communities

Now think about the Gospel of John as you have heard it and read it over the years and as it has been described here. There are certain aspects of his Gospel that are tremendously attractive to us: for example, John's emphasis on the love of God in Christ and the reality of this love in the gathered community. Jesus says in John's Gospel of the community that will gather around his name after his death, "They who have my commandments and keep them are those who love me; and those who love me will be loved by my Father, and I will love them and reveal myself to them" (John 14:21). However, like in any community, there is a dark or shadow side. John's community doesn't appear to have the tolerance of different experiences of Jesus living side by side that Mark achieves in his Gospel. With John, it is clear that some are in and some are out.

As a leader in the church, how do you feel about the way John seems to exclude individuals and make sharp distinctions between who is in the community and who is not in the community? In light of the religious pluralism of today, and especially of the marriages of people of different faiths in your own community, how do you talk about this as a congregation? How is this issue discussed with your young people and the children in your church school? How does a congregation that holds scripture in high regard engage the less appealing aspects of the life of early Christian communities?

Letting Scripture Talk: Luke's Communities

At Christmas when I was a boy growing up in the Midwest, along with decorating a tree, placing a wreath on the front door, setting out the crèche on a shelf on the staircase landing, and draping garlands of greens along the banister and on a table in the front hall, my mother would set out our family Bible open to the beginning of the second chapter of the Gospel of Luke. She placed candles next to the open Bible so everyone in our family and all who visited our home during the Christmas season would be exposed to the passage beginning with these familiar words: "In those days a decree went out from Emperor Augustus that all the world should be registered" (Luke 2:1).

My mother couldn't have chosen more wisely. For what were we? We were an ordinary family of the 1950s: three sons, a daughter, a father who went to work each day, and a mother who cared for the home. My father served on the vestry of our church, my mother taught in the Sunday school, my sister sang in the choir, and all three boys served at the altar on Sunday. We were tax-paying American citizens, and we were Christians. We were, almost two thousand years later, very much the kind of people to whom Luke was writing his Gospel.

Luke had a much broader audience in mind than did the writers of Matthew, Mark, and John, or even Paul. He wasn't writing for some small Christian communities huddled together in the northern Galilee, like John; or for the community of Matthew, somewhere in Syria, coming from a tradition of the Law; or for little house churches in Antioch, like Mark; or for particular churches in major cities of the Roman Empire, like Paul. Luke was writing his Gospel to the whole of the Roman Empire. His Gospel was for the whole world. For the angel proclaims to the shepherds concerning the birth of Jesus, "I am bringing you good news of great joy for all the people" (Luke 2:10).

Luke's Gospel is for every age. He tells us right from the beginning of his Gospel that this birth of Jesus of Nazareth is no sectarian event that happened in some lost corner of the world, affecting only a few people. Luke is saying that this is a world event that should concern every person in the world. Because of the birth of Jesus at a particular time in a particular place, all human governments are overseen by God's rule. This event will make a huge difference in human history, and it is something that will make a difference in the lives of every human being in the world, even down to the Shaw family in Coldwater, Michigan, in the 1950s.

Some scholars believe Luke to be the last of the Gospels written. Luke, who is also the author of Acts, wasn't writing to Jews who lived through the destruction of the Temple and the upheaval of the war with the Roman government. Luke was writing to people who lived in a more settled time and place, when there was more economic prosperity and security. From Acts, we learn a good deal about Luke's understanding of Christian life in the Roman Empire. For example, some of the theological disputes that so disrupted the communities to whom Paul ministered had long since been settled in certain parts of the church. Gentiles now seem fully accepted in the church; indeed, it is more than likely that the author of Luke was a Gentile. Unlike Paul or Mark, Luke doesn't appear to be threatened by the Roman government. Quite to the contrary, Luke and the readers he is trying to reach through his Gospel appear to be very much at home in the Roman Empire.

Luke identified the church community he wanted to build up as the church in the whole of the Roman Empire. His challenge was very different from those of his predecessors. He was writing to people who held down jobs, had families, owned possessions, and probably had some power in their communities. It was to these people that he says: This is how you are supposed to live, see the world, and experience power since the birth of Jesus of Nazareth. He meant to form and challenge Christians who were very much a part of their contemporary society.

In fact, Luke's challenge seems to be the reconciliation of many of the earlier church's concerns with the church of the late first or early second century. What do you preach about the coming of Jesus Christ when it is now seventy or even eighty years after his death and resurrection? How do you reconcile the wealthy person with the poor Jesus of Nazareth, who advocates so aggressively for the poor, when there are more and more wealthy people being drawn to the church during the time of Luke? How do you fashion a gospel in a period when becoming a Christian didn't necessarily mean renouncing all that you had been, as was required in earlier church communities? What do you say about Christ and Christianity, with its ancient roots and sacred texts, to a Greek-speaking population throughout the Mediterranean who seems in this settled, peaceful time to be fascinated with new religions coming from the East? These are some of the questions Luke tried to answer in his Gospel in his effort to build up the community of the church.

Because of the worldwide community nature of the church he hopes to serve, it suits Luke to be a good historian in the crafting of his Gospel. He draws on a wide variety of sources, and he attempts to set out his material in an orderly fashion through his arranging and editing of stories that he had read in Mark (or another source common to both), the material he shared with Matthew, and his other sources.

Talking about What Your Church Can Learn from Luke's Communities

Often when a parish is going through a period of discernment around calling new ordained leadership, beginning a capital campaign, constructing a new building, renovating a worship space, or dealing with some significant conflict in the life of the congregation, consultants will recommend constructing a timeline of the history of the parish. When all the pertinent information for the timeline is offered by the gathered parishioners, it is usually placed on newsprint that covers one wall of the meeting room. There it is for everyone to see: when the church moved from one geographical place to another, when the education wing was built, the date of the fire, the tenures of the clergy who have served the parish, the deaths of important members of the congregation, when worship changed or a new ministry began—it is all a chronicle of how the Holy Spirit has moved among them through the decades or centuries of their community's existence.

When the community can see how God has been present to it in the past through this kind of timeline or narrative, it can help members make decisions about their current life and how they are going to live now as a faithful community. When the people of the community can see, right in front of them, what God has done, it often gives them the courage to take risks, trusting that just as God was always present with them in the past, so, too, is God present with them now. The narrative of the past is a tool for current self-examination and gives us hope for our future.

Of course, any good consultant knows that a timeline created by church members on a weekend retreat isn't the whole story. The consultant knows that what any group remembers is selective, depending on who is present that day and the vision particular people have for the future of their church long before the conversation begins. A perceptive consultant is careful to listen to what is not being said and to whoever might not be present on that particular day. There is always a danger if a timeline is read at face value and congregational decisions are made on that basis.

The Gospel of Luke is a little like that. It's a kind of timeline of the early church, and its purpose is much like the timeline of a congregation: it helps people see where they have been and uses that information to help them live the life of their community now and into the future. Luke's timeline, his narrative, looks us straight in the eye, from every age of the church's life. And it asks: What impact do the birth, ministry, suffering, death, and resurrection of Jesus make in how you and your ordinary church fellowship live in your community and the society and culture of which you are a part?

But we have to be good consultants, real critical thinkers, when we read the Gospel of Luke and the Book of Acts. We can't just take what they say at face value. In a sense, Luke's timeline doesn't have everyone in the room, and the people who are there, especially in the Book of Acts, have a particularly rosy view of what went on in the history of the early church. If you were to read Luke and Acts straight through, you would get the idea that the church just goes from strength to strength to strength. Like a good consultant, when you read Luke and Acts, to get the full picture, you have to keep in mind the members of the church who aren't there in the room, along with the other Gospels and the writings of Paul. Still, Luke gives the ordinary Christian like you or me confidence and assurance in the advancement of the kingdom of God.

Luke asks us important questions. For example, as an ordinary individual in an ordinary Christian community, what do you do with the resource of time that God has given to you? Given the worldwide importance of this child's birth, ministry, suffering, death, and resurrection, as a believer in this decisive act of God in human history, how do you use your financial resources to promote the unfolding kingdom of God? Luke is telling us that even though we are just ordinary people, we have enormous power and insight because of the significance of Jesus' suffering, death, and resurrection. So other questions he might be asking us are: How, in the name of Jesus Christ, do we use that power politically in the world? How do we express with our civic life and voting our belief in this kingdom that continues to be manifested?

❖

Paul, Mark, Matthew, John, and Luke are all writing to very different communities in different geographical locations in very different times and to diverse populations of the Roman Empire. All of them chose and edited stories of Jesus of Nazareth from a variety of sources to meet the particular needs of the community for which they are concerned. Each of these individuals is challenging the members of their communities over their unique issues, and offering them a vision of God through the person of Jesus of Nazareth to sustain them in the ministry to which they have been called. Because they are addressing a church with particular needs in a particular context, each writer has limitations, blind spots, and prejudices, which we must take into consideration in our conversation with them. Yet, as different as they are from one another, all of them are convinced of the continuation of God's revelation in Jesus Christ in the gathered fellowship of the church. Each one in his own brilliant way is dedicated to building up the community of his church for the salvation of the world.

A Contemporary Gospel

At least one reason most of us go to church is to hear good preaching. Good preaching raises prophetic issues, contains good teaching on scripture, and is able to connect the life of faith with the world in which we live. If your rector takes preaching seriously, I bet that if she has been with you for five years or more, and you had the time to sit down and read through all of her sermons from that period, one right after the other, a kind of gospel written to your particular church would emerge for you. It would be kind of like the Gospel of Sam, or Cathy, or Annie. You would begin to see how your rector, because she has such a keen awareness of your particular congregation, uses certain themes or stories from the New Testament each Sunday, how she shapes and fashions them in a very precise way, to speak directly to you and to build up the life of your particular community.

I hope you have seen in these first two chapters that it was a little like that for Paul, Mark, Matthew, John, and Luke. They knew their churches, and they knew what themes, stories, and teachings of Jesus of Nazareth would build up their communities. They then fashioned that material and crafted it in a way that the message of Jesus Christ could be heard by their congregations.

Could you now have a conversation around some of the issues your church is facing in your life together? For example, you talk to me a lot about money and giving to the church. You often speak to me of conflict in your church or in the wider church. Often you ask me about how other churches attract new members, and you ask about the role worship should play in your life together. You tell me about the lack of time in your personal life and the demands you often feel your church community makes on you and other members. Sometimes when I listen to you, I hear despair over the homelessness in our country, war, the devastation caused by natural disasters, and the lack of response to those disasters by our government, and you express concern over the suffering caused by worldwide epidemics, like HIV/AIDS, and developing (or Third World) ones like malaria. How do we respond to so much suffering? you ask me. Where do we find a message of hope?

Time, hope, suffering, worship, evangelism, giving, conflict, and outreach were all familiar themes to the churches of the New Testament. Paul, Matthew, Mark, Luke, and John all wrote to their congregations on these subjects. In these next chapters, listen to how these communities spoke of these issues through their commitment to Jesus Christ. Speak to one another, through your faith in Jesus Christ, of what you think God is saying to your congregation. There are no answers in these chapters. Any answers, any ways you find to strengthen your leadership and your church, will come through your conversation with each other and the conversation you have with scripture.

CHAPTER THREE

The Cross and Suffering of Jesus

NOT LONG AGO, in a conversation with a college sophomore, she reminded me that, after going through confirmation classes at her church while she was in high school,
she had decided not to be confirmed when the time came for a visitation in her parish. It wasn't that she thought the church was irrel-
evant. That wasn't the case for her. In fact, even though she attends a
university with no Episcopal chaplaincy and her school friends don't
go to church, most Sunday mornings she gets out of bed and goes
to the local parish. She loves going to church. She enjoys the service
and the singing. Because the other six days of the week she is with
people her age most of the time, it is important for her, on this one
day, to be with everyone, from children to octogenarians. But most
of all, her reason for going to church is because she loves and
respects the teachings of Jesus. "I just don't know, Tom, if I believe
all the rest of it, like Jesus on the cross and the resurrection," she said.

There are a lot of people like her in the Episcopal Church, people who are attracted to our denomination because of the ritual, the
music, our respect for the integrity of the person's individual spiritual journey, or our active engagement with ethical and moral issues.
Or, like the college student, they are simply drawn to the teachings

of Jesus. They don't assent to everything in the Nicene Creed, in scripture, or in the tradition of the church. No matter how much or how little these people believe, I like it when they all stay. I am proud that we have such permeable borders in the Episcopal Church.

Letting Scripture Talk

There is every reason to believe that the churches founded or nurtured by Paul likewise had permeable borders. While Paul may have had strong opinions about cultural issues particular to his day, he seems to have encouraged a good deal of latitude in belief and commitment in the congregations he served. He wasn't quick to say who was considered a member of the church and who was considered not part of the church. As a matter of fact, Paul thought it was important to cast a broad net and just see who was attracted to Christ and his body, the church. Let whoever wants to come, come, is what Paul seems to be saying to the church. Then let the chips fall where they may.

What Paul hoped these permeable borders would do is attract Jews and Gentiles, for whatever reason, to the forming church. Then, through the witness of the gathered church, the shared meal, the teaching, and the ministry, they would be drawn to the richest possible place, the very core of our faith and experience of Jesus Christ: his suffering, death, and resurrection. Regardless of what initially drew people to these little house churches, Paul knew that if, through participating in the fellowship, they could be grasped by the power of the suffering, crucifixion, and resurrection, then they would know the full freedom of what it is to live in Christ. Paul knew how strong those congregations in Philippi, Galatia, Rome, or Thessalonica would be if their members truly lived from the suffering, death, and resurrection of Jesus Christ.

What did the suffering and death of our Lord Jesus Christ mean to the very diverse Christian communities spread out across the Roman Empire, living at different times, coming from very different traditions? It is an important question for us to ask because, despite all their variety, for Paul, Matthew, Mark, Luke, and John, the suffering and death of Jesus were at the heart of their gathered life.

There is remarkable congruity in the four Gospels around the actual trial and death of Jesus of Nazareth. All four tell of Jesus praying with his disciples before his arrest. In all four he appears before the council. They all tell of Peter's denial, the criminal Barabbas, Jesus being tried before Pilate, the taking up of his cross, and his death. Given how different the Gospels are because of the specific needs of the communities for which they were written, this kind of agreement tells us at least how central this part of the story is to every Christian community in every age. In fact, these writers' inclusion of the passion and death of Jesus of Nazareth and their faithfulness to the story being told are most likely the reason these four Gospels—and the letters of Paul—were chosen out of the scores of writings circulating in the early church for what we now call the New Testament.

The authors of the four Gospels so wanted their communities to understand the importance of the passion and death of Jesus that, long before they get to that part of their story, they have Jesus warn his followers that these painful events will be the end of all his teaching, preaching, and healing. In Matthew and Mark, Jesus prepares his disciples by telling them on three separate occasions of his coming crucifixion. Luke, in his narrative, foretells the death of Jesus numerous times. Even John, different as his Gospel is from those of Matthew, Mark, and Luke, speaks of the coming suffering and death of Jesus. Paul, in writing to the communities for which he was responsible, again and again speaks of the centrality of the death of Jesus on the cross to the witness of the Christian life (I Corinthians 1:23–25).

Paul and, I think, the authors of the Gospels would have had enormous empathy for my young friend who told me she just can't believe everything. If she had lived in the first or early second century in some place like Antioch or Philippi, I believe she would have been welcomed into their communities. After all, their little house churches seemed to have been made up of Jews and Gentiles with very different reasons for being part of these communities and different understandings and experiences of who Jesus of Nazareth was. I expect they would have found a place for this questioning college sophomore.

And yet, it appears, they would have made it clear to a seeker who joined them that the whole point of their being together was the central mystery of the suffering, death, and resurrection of Jesus Christ. The purpose of all the teaching, the discussion, the preaching, and prayer of these house churches was to reveal the mystery of redemption through the offering of Christ on the cross. The whole of their fellowship would have been an invitation to a seeker, whether Jew or Gentile, to go deeper and deeper, through the gathered life of the community, until the seeker was embraced by this central truth. This mystery was the heart of God's revelation to humanity, and finally, the way to God for all of them was through this mystery.

But remember how different Mark's house churches in Antioch in the 60s CE were from John's communities living in the northern Galilee thirty or forty years later. Think of how different Paul's forming fellowships of Jews and Gentiles in major cities around the Mediterranean before the destruction of the Temple in Jerusalem in 70 CE were from Matthew's churches in Syria well after that. Remember how distinct Luke's message is to his congregations spread across the Roman Empire in the late first or early second century. Because these congregations were so different from one another in location, time, circumstances, and membership, each of the Gospel writers and Paul used the suffering and death of Jesus Christ in a different way to build up their congregations. Let's look at how Mark and John did this.

The Gospel of Mark Talks about the Cross

We were off for our afternoon run along the Charles River, Brother James and I, when a large black patch on the back of his calf caught my eye. "What is that?" I asked, pointing to his leg. We stopped running as he twisted his leg around to get a look at his calf. "It's a mole," he responded. "I'm Irish. We have moles. It's been there for awhile." "That's more than a mole," I said. "You should get a doctor to look at it." "I will," he vaguely promised, "but believe me, there's no need to worry. Remember, I'm Irish."

So every time we went running together, I let myself look at whatever it was on his leg, I forced myself not to worry. I could tell he was forcing himself not to worry, too, because on those rare occasions when I did ask if he had made an appointment, he was understandably defensive. Why would James or any of us in the community have wanted to know the truth about that dark patch on the back of his leg? He was a talented young man, with years and years of valuable ministry ahead of him. Life in our community at that time, while it certainly had its challenges, was basically good. Why rock the boat with potentially bad news?

In spite of this initial avoidance, James did go to the doctor. He came home with terrible news: stage four melanoma. One afternoon in those bleak days immediately following the diagnosis and his first surgery, he told me he was actually relieved to know the truth after living with the avoidance and uncertainty of the previous months. "Now with this diagnosis," he said to me, "I know what I am up against and the fight I have on my hands." And fight he did.

In retrospect, I can see that all of us in our monastic community, his family, and friends fought together with James over the long, long journey from his cancer diagnosis in his mid-twenties until his death in his late thirties. Throughout all the remissions, operations, symptoms, hospitalizations, and recurrences of the melanoma, we fought best together when we knew what we were up against. When we knew the truth, we took the best care of James and each other, our prayer was most honest, and we were best able to receive the grace God was offering to us in this difficult time. I think that is true of all of us. My experience as a pastor tells me that most of us do our best when we know the truth, even if it is hard and difficult. The whole truth allows us to act with integrity.

That seems to be the sense of the author of the Gospel of Mark as well. There is no doubt about the fact that his Gospel is meant to be good news for those house churches in Antioch. After all, the first words of his first chapter are, "The beginning of the good news of

Jesus Christ, the Son of God." For the truth of this Gospel is, with the coming of Jesus of Nazareth, the kingdom of God has been inaugurated. Mark is clear that a new day has dawned in human history. The preaching and the teaching, the stories, the miracles, and the healings of Jesus are all manifestations of the reality that the kingdom of God has come. Mark wants his congregations to know that this new age is a time for joy and celebration. He communicates this on every page of his Gospel.

Just think of the impact this good news would have had upon those partly Jewish, partly Gentile communities of believers in Jesus. Here they were, most likely displaced people from the Galilee or Jerusalem or Syria, in an unfamiliar place, coming to know Jesus Christ through different teachers, different oral traditions, different personal experiences of God, and through different religions or strands of Judaism. Think of the unifying potential of Mark's good news if all these little communities, so different from one another, were now telling the same stories, acting out the same drama of the proclamation of the kingdom of God in Jesus of Nazareth, or reading the same words of their salvation. Think how this shared Gospel would strengthen their life together, help them remind one another of all that Jesus did, and give them a sense of a common purpose.

You can imagine as well how Mark's Gospel might invigorate their ministry. Given the urgency with which Jesus seems to do everything in this Gospel, it is easy to see how they would be motivated by this text to get going now with their healing, teaching, and caring for the disenfranchised. As hearers of Mark's Gospel, they understood that because of the death and resurrection of Jesus Christ, they were now the agents of this dawning kingdom of God. Mark's words must have been important to the building up of their life together and of their ministry beyond their congregations.

True as this talk might have been for Mark's communities, this talk of a dawning kingdom of God and therefore a vibrant service to the forgotten of the world—it wasn't the whole truth. And Mark knew that they would never survive as congregations and would never flourish in their ministry unless they were aware of the full truth. He wants their eyes wide open.

So he goes about exposing his congregations to the full truth, and he does this with such dramatic skill that he is adapted by the later Gospel writers in the New Testament. It is clear that Matthew and Luke were not only aware of Mark's Gospel but held Mark in such high regard that they used many of the stories and parables of Jesus that Mark had collected.

For what happens in the unfolding of Mark's extraordinary story of the good news of Jesus Christ? Life was being transformed. In Jesus thousands who were hungry were now being fed. The blind were being given their sight, and the ears of the deaf were being opened. In stories like the healing of the Syrophoenician woman's daughter, Jesus radically shatters religious and gender boundaries (Mark 7:24–29). Yet in the midst of all this good news, Jesus tells his disciples he is going to suffer and die. On three separate occasions, he reminds his followers of this (Mark 8:31, 9:31 & 10:32–34). His miracles, teachings, and healings, the very acts that proclaim his ushering in of the kingdom of God, also expose the religious and civic leaders as the oppressors they are. Jesus is on a collision course with the recognized authority. He is speaking out against the status quo, and for doing this, he will pay with his life.

Mark knows a thing or two about human nature. He knows, as his listeners hear the remarkable stories of transformation, as they themselves experience their own transformation through Christ's risen presence in their communities, how easy it would be in the midst of all this joy to lose sight of or even deny the suffering and death of Jesus, which is the inevitable outcome of his radical behavior. What does Mark do to refute this very natural tendency to deny suffering? Into the midst of his unfolding story, he carefully inserts the responses of Peter and the other disciples, who, like their fellow followers of Jesus thirty or forty years later in Antioch, also didn't want to hear of Jesus' passion and death.

Given that Jesus so clearly embodies the love and justice of God, given his popularity and their love for him, you can see why his disciples in any age don't want to believe Jesus will suffer and die (Mark 8:32 & 9:32). Who among us would have wanted such a life as the first disciples had with Jesus, such a life full of promise and hope, to be spoiled by a prediction of death? Who among us experiencing the joy of transformation and hope for an unfolding kingdom would be drawn to remember it?

There is more to it than that Jesus will suffer and die. By saying, "If any want to become my followers, let them deny themselves and take up their cross and follow me. For those who want to save their life will lose it…" (Mark 8:34–35), Mark is warning the disciples of those house churches in Antioch that as they participate in the proclamation of the kingdom of God through their preaching, healing, and casting out of demons, they will also participate in the suffering of Jesus.

Central to Mark's message about this inevitable suffering was word of its transformative power. All suffering, whether it is personal or on behalf of others, carries with it the possibility of transformation. Were there some in Mark's congregations who were so caught up in the proclamation of the kingdom that they were resisting the suffering that is part of the truth of Jesus' life? Was the resistance to suffering, which the Jesus of Mark says comes with caring for the disenfranchised, somehow weakening the life of those congregations? Were some refusing to accept their responsibilities in serving the outcasts who were so important to Mark's Jesus? Did some of these followers not want the whole truth of what it was to be part of a fellowship of believers?

Mark thought that if they could embrace the whole of what it is to be a follower of Jesus Christ, including the cross and suffering for others, they would be a community united and bold in the unfolding of the kingdom of God, of which they were a part. Having the whole truth made them stronger. It is a truth meant to build community for the ministry of the Gospel.

Talking about What Your Church Can Learn from Mark about the Cross

How could Mark's understanding of the cross and death of Jesus and the way he used his understanding to build up the forming churches in Antioch apply to your congregation?

You might begin your discussion this way: Many of us have had the experience of suffering through an addiction, a divorce or broken relationship, a long illness, the loss of a job, or the death of someone we love. While it was an excruciatingly painful experience for us, we also know that going through this suffering has transformed us. We are different people because of this experience. Some of us might even say we are stronger or better because of it. Could you share with one another some of the transformation you have experienced through suffering?

Now shift the discussion to your congregation. In the history of your congregation, can you identify any times of intense suffering? The suffering might have been caused by some inappropriate conduct of your ordained leadership or by a disaster, like a fire or flood, recovery from which seemed to sap the energy from your parish, or it could have been a particular stance the people of your parish took on some controversial issue in your city that has caused your suffering. As you discuss this suffering, are you aware of any ways God transformed your community through it? How are you stronger now as a congregation? Are you able to be more honest with one another? Are you more willing to take on difficult tasks or issues that may cause suffering or sacrifice for your congregation because you know of the transformative power of suffering?

Can you identify any places of suffering in your church right now? How do you talk about this difficult reality with one another? Do you pray about it together? Because you know from your personal as well as communal experience of how painful suffering can be, do you think there are ways your church is avoiding suffering and the gift of transformation that is part of suffering in Jesus Christ? As leaders of your congregation, how willing are you to explore and share the transformative power of suffering with the rest of your brothers and sisters in Christ? Do you ever, as the spiritual leaders of your church, talk to one another about the risks the Jesus of Mark is asking his followers to make on his behalf? If not, why not? Do you ever let God express God's gratitude for the suffering you have taken on as a congregation on behalf of Jesus Christ?

The Gospel of John Talks about the Cross

Like the worship life of the community of your congregation, the heart of the monastic community where I have lived for the past thirty years is the celebration of Holy Week and Easter. These services are so important to our life in our monastic community that a few days after Holy Week and Easter, we begin planning next year's celebration. The closer we get to Holy Week, the more time we spend preparing homilies, rehearsing music, perfecting the liturgy, and preparing the chapel. As you can imagine, with a group of twenty-five or so strong-willed men who care deeply about the celebration of these events critical to our faith, sometimes the preparations can be so intense that sleep is lost and tempers are frayed.

After listening to many of you over the years, I believe it is like this for you in your communities as well. Whether you are in a large or small parish, you begin planning Holy Week long before it occurs. You rehearse music, the altar guild prepares for the services, your worship committee and the rector plan the liturgies, service bulletins need to be produced: many, many parishioners are engaged in getting ready for these days, which are so central to the story of our redemption through our Lord Jesus Christ. You often tell me that there are conflicting ideas among various groups in your parish about how liturgies should be celebrated in Holy Week and what music is appropriate for the occasion. Like our monastic community, those of you who are involved in your parish Holy Week planning tell me that because everyone cares so deeply about these services, there is often friction, misunderstanding, and a concern that everything that needs to be done won't get done by Palm Sunday.

Whether it is a monastic community like mine or a parish community like yours, with elaborate or very simple Holy Week celebrations, I know that once we actually begin the liturgies of Holy Week, the Spirit moves among us, and we are drawn deeper and deeper into the reality of this profound mystery of our redemption. As we share in the liturgies of Maundy Thursday, Good Friday, and Holy Saturday, we experience an immeasurable unity with one another through the magnificence of God's love for each of us through the sacrifice of Jesus Christ.

I will never forget one of my first Good Fridays as a monk. Our monastery chapel was packed. There were students and faculty from nearby colleges and universities, divinity students from a variety of denominations, neighbors, people we had never seen before in our chapel, and those who were part of our regular worshipping community. The congregation was old and young, people of color, white people, men and women, some who were physically disabled, overweight people and thin people, some whom I knew to be chronically depressed, some who had recently converted to Christianity, others who had been practicing Christians for seventy or eighty years, and some, I suspected, who had the most tenuous experience of faith. In other words, the whole people of God seemed to be present.

We had heard the lessons, our community choir had sung with great beauty the account of the passion from St. John's Gospel, and we had chanted the solemn collects. It was time now for the veneration of the cross. The celebrant of the liturgy, the deacon, and the subdeacon processed from the back of the chapel, with a wooden cross, stopping three times, lifting the cross high in the air, each time the deacon singing, "Behold the wood of the cross." After they had reverently placed the cross on a cushion on the floor in front of the altar, the three ministers returned to the back of the chapel, and each one came forward again, stopping three times, dropping to their knees, and bowing until their heads touched the floor. As each one came to the cross, he knelt to kiss it, all the while the choir singing a polyphonic anthem.

Then it was the turn of the rest of the congregation to venerate the cross. We expected people to form an orderly line, rather like they were going forward to receive communion, kneel down at the cross, touch it or kiss it, and then return to their seats. But that isn't what happened. Instead, in pairs, most total strangers to each other, in imitation of the ministers, they knelt three times as they progressed to the cross, touching their foreheads to the marble floor before kissing the cross. "This," I thought impatiently to myself, "is going to take forever. We won't get out of here until ten p.m."

Too agitated to pray, I watched the pairs moving slowly to the front of the chapel. They were people of different shapes, degrees of agility, and, presumably, temperaments, often offering the other a hand in assistance as they got up from their knees, making their way to the cross. It came to me then, that passage from St. John's Gospel, "And I, when I am lifted up from the earth, will draw all people to myself" (John 12:32). The more I watched, the more it became clear to me that as different as these people were from one another, they were all profoundly attracted to the love God had shown for them on the cross. The more I watched them as they knelt, bowed, and struggled back to their feet, the more aware I became of the deep gratitude on their part for this God who suffered for their salvation. There was a kind of abandonment of self on the part of the worshippers to the love they experienced in the cross. As each individual in the pair bent to kiss the cross, we all seemed to go deeper and deeper into our unity in Christ.

In the end, I think I could have watched this veneration for hours. Through the devotion of the people in the congregation to the cross, I went from being agitated about the time this was taking and disgruntled with the member of the community who hadn't foreseen this complication, to experiencing a deep contentment. I was happy simply being with these people. I wanted to be there on that evening with that gathered community more than any place else in the world. As I let myself experience the contentment, the Spirit gave me another passage from St. John's Gospel, "Abide in me as I abide in you" (John 15:4). "Oh," I thought to myself, "this is why John, when he writes to those communities in the late first century, uses the word *abide* forty times in his Gospel. He knew how deep their sense of contentment, happiness, and unity could be if together they reflected on the passion and cross of Jesus."

For the author of John's Gospel, the suffering and death of Jesus on the cross were the supreme revelation of God's love for him and for those formerly Jewish communities, now believers in Jesus, to whom he ministered. Remember, these were devout people who had been deeply affected by the wisdom and mystical tradition in Judaism. They had most likely been thrown out of their synagogues because they believed Jesus to be the Son of God. It could be that for one reason or another, some of their former members had deserted them. They felt themselves to be under some kind of threat. They had to be certain of the constancy of God.

The suffering and cross of Jesus became the sign of God's constancy for them. This community to whom John wrote had had decades to pray about Jesus' death. They had pored over scripture, trying to discern the meaning of this event, and then, most likely, they had discussed amongst themselves what his death meant for them individually and corporately. Their understanding of the suffering and death of Jesus of Nazareth was much more subtle or nuanced than Mark's understanding of the cross, which we examined earlier in this chapter. Mark, you remember, wanted the house churches to which he wrote to understand the inevitability of suffering for those who followed Jesus and the transformative power of that suffering. John wanted the men and women to whom he wrote to understand that Jesus' death on the cross wasn't a defeat or the inevitable outcome of a public ministry that challenged the religious authority of the day. Instead, it was an event that revealed the true nature of God's love: humble, sacrificial, and self-emptying. Here was a God so constant, so present to them, that God was willing to take on the whole of human existence, even suffering and death, which are part of all of our lives. God was so constant that God, in Jesus, was willing to give all that God had for every one of them. The cross was God at God's most beautiful.

This model of God's faithfulness to humankind in the suffering of the cross became the inspiration for the way these early Christians related to each other in their community of the church. Surely, because this was a gathering of human beings, there must have been issues that divided them: personality differences, theological differences, and practical matters of running the community. But this love God expressed through Jesus Christ on the cross was so attractive that when they meditated on it, celebrated it in a common meal, and talked about it, the cross drew them together and gave them a unity that seemed to break through anything that might separate them. This knowledge of the cross deepened and strengthened their community. How could the members of this community not be vulnerable to one another faced with such vulnerability of God? How could they possibly attempt to exert power over one another in the face of this kind of humility exhibited by their God? The cross made it possible for them to trust one another, listen for the Spirit in one another, and sacrifice for one another. Most of all, the cross made it possible for them to abide with one another in the kingdom of God.

For them, the suffering and death of Jesus on the cross made present the kingdom of God in their fellowship right now. The kingdom, John says to them, is not something that is coming and will be experienced at a later date; it is here and present to us now as we abide and live with one another right here at the end of the first century in the northern part of the Galilee. Remain here in this community and you will experience the fullness of God through the cross of Jesus Christ. As the author of John's Gospel says to his listeners over and over again, the Son abides in the Father, and because of the cross, we abide in him and he abides in us. John speaks this same message to us living in the communities of our congregations and monasteries in the twenty-first century.

Talking about What Your Church Can Learn from John about the Cross

Our cathedral is right in the center of downtown Boston. It is a rather unobtrusive building set back from the street. Our worshipping congregation is usually small for such a large space. But it isn't a small congregation on Good Friday, from 12:00 p.m. to 3:00 p.m. The pews are practically full. People come in during their lunch hour; others stay for the full three hours. Many of those who attend we have never seen before at the cathedral. It is obvious that many are not Episcopalians, and clearly, some have not been to church for a very long time. What is it about this day that draws so many people to worship?

I believe people gather in churches on Good Friday because they are compelled on this day to adore this God who loves them so much. I believe they sense that if anything represents real unity and humility in this troubled and divided world, it is the lifting up of Jesus on the cross. The cross seems to quench an unbearable thirst.

Can you begin your discussion of how John's understanding of the cross might build up your congregation by sharing with one another how you personally are drawn to the suffering and death of Jesus? Is it that you are in awe of a God who loves with such abandonment of self? Are you deeply moved by a God who would make this sacrifice for you? Do you see yourself, as John's Gospel portrays the Beloved Disciple and Mary Magdalene, as one who stands at the foot of the cross, witnessing to this remarkable love of God through the suffering and death of Jesus? Or do you resist this complete self-emptying of Jesus and somehow see it as unimportant to your belief in God? Do you see yourself as John saw Peter and the other disciples of Jesus who ran away from the suffering of the cross?

Now shift your discussion to church. Sometimes when I listen to you in congregational and leadership meetings, it sounds to me as though you feel like your parish could be under threat. You tell me there is not much in today's culture that supports the community of faith. People work on Sundays, and there are sports for kids on Sundays: the lack of time to volunteer, the consumerism of contemporary Western society, and the skewed values people hold all seem to undermine the life of the church. How could the message of John's understanding of the cross, with his emphasis on vulnerability, trust, and powerlessness, build your church?

Do you ever talk about how you exert power in your families, in the workplace, or in the church? How could you, as leaders, model these values for the rest of the church membership? How could you invite people into this kind of community and experience the kingdom of God right here and now in your church? Share with one another a time, no matter how brief the moment, when you have experienced the reality of the kingdom of God in the fellowship of your vestry or your church.

CHAPTER

FOUR

The Resurrection

"DO YOU really believe," the local television anchor-woman asked me, "that one ten-day trip such as you made with your group is going to bring peace to the Middle East?" It was early in the second intifada, and I had just returned with a group of Episcopalians from the West Bank and Israel, where we had witnessed firsthand the destruction by the Israeli military in Bethlehem and in the Jenin Refugee Camp. "No," I replied, "I am not that naïve. But I do believe peace will come if everyone does their part. In the great human and civil rights movements in history, it isn't just one person that brings about change; it is thousands of ordinary people struggling for justice over a long period of time. I am hopeful."

Several years have passed since that interview. In the intervening time, I have accompanied fellow bishops, lay people from across the United States, clergy, and college students to the West Bank and Israel to raise consciousness concerning the war between Palestine and Israel. I have participated in demonstrations, given speeches, written op-ed pieces, and lobbied in Congress concerning peace in the Middle East. I have sponsored events to teach people about what is happening in that part of the world. I have helped raise money for schools and housing in the West Bank and for human rights groups in Israel. I have participated in dialogues with my Jewish brothers and sisters, and I have listened to countless stories of Christian and Muslim Palestinians and Israeli Jews.

There are hundreds of thousands of people around the globe who are working and praying for peace in the Middle East, and yet the situation seems to worsen every day. On each trip I make to that region, I am sadder than on the one before. After all these years of suicide bombings and incursions, people on both sides of the Wall are less safe and less free than they were ten years ago. Do I really believe what I said in the television interview about hope?

What do we believe about hope for our own lives? No matter how well intentioned we are about living lives of wholeness and fulfillment, most of us recognize continuing patterns of self-destructive behavior or sinfulness in our lives. For one person, this self-destructive behavior might be an angry temper; for another, it might be extreme dependence on others for happiness; or for another, it might be the way they isolate themselves from the love people offer. Whatever it is, no matter how hard the individual attempts to confront the behavior, it seems it is always there, undermining the person's sense of wholeness and dignity. It feels to that person that he or she is always going to be imprisoned or held back by this self-destructive behavior. How can one, then, retain hope in the possibility of a new life?

I think of a friend I have who is addicted to sex. It is an addiction not unlike perhaps more familiar addictions to alcohol, drugs, gambling, and food. For a long time now, it has been almost impossible for my friend to overcome a compulsion to have sex, most often with people he doesn't know and has little interest in ever meeting again. He goes to meetings to help him in recovery from his addiction to sex. He has a therapist. He prays and goes to church regularly, and he has supportive friends. He has gone for months at a time without having anonymous sex, but when he does slip, it is terrible for him. His confidence dissolves, his self-esteem is destroyed, and he loses hope of recovering from this addiction.

Perhaps your loss of hope is not as profound as the feeling you have when you are caught yet again in a pattern of self-destructive behavior, or as dramatic as the loss of hope my friend has after he slips. But sometimes you tell me you are ready to give up hope over the unity of our international Anglican Communion. How long have we been struggling with division in the Anglican Communion? Too long, you often tell me. All the litigation, the statements on behalf of one part of the church or another, and the sensationalist media coverage, you say, sap energy for mission and evangelism. Why can't there be some resolution? Why can't we get on with the work of the gospel? With all the other struggles congregations face, you tell me, you have just about given up hope in the institution of the church.

Letting Scripture Talk about the Resurrection

I wonder if there were some people in those house churches in Corinth so dear to Paul who likewise had just about given up hope by the time they wrote to him around 54 CE. We don't actually have the letter they wrote to Paul, but from Paul's response to them, we can figure out some of what was threatening those little congregations. Because Paul's churches invited everyone, from the very rich to the very poor, the educated as well as the illiterate, differences in class began to emerge as the congregation gathered for a meal and for worship. Unlike the potlucks we have in our churches, where everyone shares, it seems that in the congregations in Corinth, you ate what you brought. The poor of the community, it looks like, often had nothing to eat at the meal. "For when the time comes to eat," Paul writes, "each of you goes ahead with your own supper, and one goes hungry and another becomes drunk" (I Corinthians 11:21).

There is a lot that seems to be fracturing the life of this community and impeding its unity in the proclamation of Jesus Christ. Apparently, because Paul encouraged people from all different kinds of religious backgrounds to join the fellowship, some individuals thought they had a greater wisdom or knowledge of God than others (I Corinthians 3:18–20). Then Chloe, a member of the church in Corinth, and her friends reported to Paul that there were quarrels between various factions, each group wanting control over the others (I Corinthians 1:10–1). Someone else from

Corinth communicated to Paul while he was staying in Ephesus that there was sexual immorality going on in the Corinthian fellowship (I Corinthians 5:1). It also appears that there had been a lack of sensitivity on the part of some of the members towards others around the issue of eating food that had been sacrificed to idols. Sure, he tells this group, it is probably all right to eat this food, but there is more to the issue than whether it is right or wrong. Christian conduct, Paul says, must always take into consideration the feelings of all the members of the gathered church. It isn't enough, as far as Paul is concerned, just to be theologically correct about an issue (I Corinthians 8:3–13).

There is at least one more group in the Corinthian church that Paul felt, if its views were accepted by others, would be particularly destructive to the life of this forming community. In fact, if this group's views were eventually to hold sway, its understanding of the Christian life could undermine the full power of God's hopeful message to the world in the death and resurrection of Jesus Christ. Ironically, this group of Corinthians appears to have been the most positive of the various factions in the church to whom Paul was writing. What was this group promoting? According to Paul's letter, these people thought they were already reigning with Christ in all his glory. "Already," he writes to them, "you have all you want! Already you have become rich! Quite apart from us you have become kings! Indeed, I wish that you had become kings so that we might be kings with you!" (I Corinthians 4:8).

For certain, these people believed Christ had been raised from the dead, but because of Christ's resurrection, the fullness of Christ's glory had now come. The way they figured it, at the last day, there wasn't going to be any general resurrection in which all of humankind participated. The Holy Spirit was with them now. Essentially, they believed that this is as good as it gets. They didn't need to hope for anything more.

I have known some men and women like this. Often, they are committed church members who have had full and productive lives, with a certain amount of privilege. God is giving all this bounty now to us. Why should we expect more? is their attitude. They don't need a resurrection or a heavenly banquet for themselves.

While I appreciate their sense of fulfillment, if this kind of twenty-first-century Christian is anything like the first-century Christians to whom Paul was writing, then I agree with Paul that they have a very limited notion of what God has set in motion through the suffering, death, and resurrection of Jesus Christ. Paul says this group is thinking way too small, and he shows them the logical implication of what they profess to believe. "If there is no resurrection of the dead, then Christ has not been raised, then our proclamation has been in vain and your faith has been in vain" (I Corinthians 15:13–14).

Paul wrote to them to expand their vision of the resurrection. He wanted to give them real hope. Writes Paul, "If for this life only we have hoped in Christ, we are of all people most to be pitied" (I Corinthians 15:19). What this event means for you as individuals, for your church, for the world, indeed, for the whole cosmos, Paul is saying, is that nothing at any place or at any time will be the same. Death and decay no longer have any hold over any of us. With the resurrection of Jesus Christ, a new day has dawned in history, and the old pattern no longer exists. All things are made new forever. Paul knows that if they—and if we—could wrap their minds around this reality of Christ's resurrection, their lives would become suffused with hope.

Unlike the group he addresses in the eighth and the fifteenth chapters of I Corinthians, Paul doesn't believe we are anywhere near the fulfillment of reigning with Christ in glory. As wonderful and full as life in the Spirit is now, because of the death and resurrection of Jesus Christ, it is only going to get better and better. He sees the victory over sin, decay, and death as unfolding, perhaps slowly, but always moving forward to the final consummation of all things in God. "We know," he writes to the churches in Rome, "that the whole creation has been groaning in labor pain until now; and not only the creation, but we ourselves who have the first fruits of the Spirit, groan inwardly while we wait for adoption, the redemption of our bodies" (Romans 8:22–23).

Try to imagine what grasping this reality of the resurrection of Jesus Christ would mean to the strengthening of that Corinthian congregation. It would mean that this little community would be able to live now into what the world was becoming. Right there, in their congregation in Corinth, as they worshipped and shared the meal together, they could enjoy the first fruits of the resurrection. They could relate to one another and to the world in a new way because sin and death no longer had any hold on them. Oh, if they only realized that they were already free from all that bound them or divided them in the past.

Paul says if you are someone who is quarrelsome, envious, or actually likes dissension and factions in community life, you just don't have to live like that, thanks to the gift of the Holy Spirit given to us through the death and resurrection of Jesus Christ. Paul is telling the members of the Galatian congregations of this new power they have been given, if only they will use it. By contrast, he wants people in the churches in Galatia to know that they have been given in the Spirit, "...love, joy, peace, patience, kindness, generosity, faithfulness, gentleness, and self-control" (Galatians 5:22–23). It would mean not only that they held one understanding of the resurrection in common with Paul, but also that the knowledge of this reality would radicalize how they lived in the present and what they might expect in the future. The resurrection of Jesus Christ was just the beginning. From Christ's victory, this new reality was already spreading and would continue to spread to the far reaches of the world, and the cosmos. The future would hold endless possibility for them. This knowledge meant a believer in Christ could look into the deepest, darkest places of his or her own life, the lives of others, any terrible, seemingly overwhelmingly painful place in the world, and know that it was shot through with the possibility of new life and hope.

Try to imagine how such full knowledge of the resurrection might compel these Corinthian Christians to spread this good news of Christ's victory over death. If they were experiencing a freedom from destructive patterns of behavior in their own lives because of the power of Christ's resurrection, if they were finding new ways of relating to people in their church from whom they would normally be separated, if Christ's resurrection had transformed the way they lived with their anxiety caused by the oppression of the Roman Empire, if they expected a different world in the future, where God's love would reign, then surely, they had a powerful message for the rest of the world.

But unlike the misguided members of the Corinthian church, Paul railed against those who didn't believe in the resurrection, because they thought they already had the full life of the Spirit now. Those who did embrace Christ's resurrection did so through the reality of the suffering and death on the cross. The believers in the resurrection knew that because of the cross and the unfolding nature of Christ's glory, there could be no superficial celebration of the Spirit. The true believers in the resurrection knew there were no easy answers, no quick fixes, and no certain paths for the difficulties and setbacks in life. God, through the suffering, death, and resurrection of Jesus Christ, had given them a realistic hope for themselves and for the world: a knowledge that their mortality, the difficult places they found in their lives, and even hopelessness itself were the doorway into the resurrection life.

If I could somehow call into my century those first-century Corinthian Christians to whom Paul was writing, the ones who didn't believe in the fullness of the resurrection, I would want to tell them of a vision I had of the final consummation of all things in God through Jesus Christ. It goes something like this.

In one of our small, struggling parishes in a working-class neighborhood, there is a group of women with whom I meet whenever I visit there. I love to listen to these women. They are all in their eighties now. These are the women who have held this parish together for decades. Because they know how important vestries, officers, church suppers, and annual parish fairs are to the community life of the parish, they will always be the ones who volunteer at the annual meeting if no other hands go up. They are the pastoral heart of this parish, remembering birthdays, checking to see if someone is all right when they haven't been in church for a few Sundays, and making and delivering the casseroles when someone is ill. They still serve on the altar guild and show up on Sunday to sing in the dwindling choir, because of their love of worship.

They meet once every two weeks for Bible study. They admit they don't do a lot of studying; mostly they gather to support each other in old age. These women have had hard lives. They have been waitresses, nurses' aides in hospitals, and have had husbands leave them, forcing them to raise children on their own. Sometimes they have had to endure long layoffs from work with the husbands who stayed. They have lost children, and on occasion they have raised grandchildren. They don't complain. They just like to gather regularly and talk about what it is like to get old, listen to one another, occasionally give advice, and pray for one another.

At one meeting, on a cold Sunday, late into a January afternoon, they told me how hard the winters are for them now. They don't get out as much as they used to, because they are too old to shovel snow. In summer it is harder for them to be attentive to their small gardens. They just can't get down on their knees any longer to pull the weeds. It is a happy day for them, but a very, very long day, when they have the care of one of their grandchildren or great grandchildren. And yet, one of the oldest members of the group said, "You know, Tom, we don't think of ourselves as old. In our minds we are still young. It's just our bodies that are old."

With a smile and a warmth spreading all through me, I thought about these women as I drove home in the early evening. I thought of their good cheer in spite of difficult lives, the wisdom they had garnered from their personal tragedies, their trust of one another, and their love of their church. I remembered the deep lines etched in their faces, the gnarled hands, the crooked fingers, and the swollen knuckles; how they had borne the suffering of their lives in their bodies. Then I saw them. They were in heaven. Dancing. They were young and yet wise with all the decades of their living. They danced with all the exuberance of women in their twenties, and yet their bodies still showed their years of suffering.

Just then, for a few minutes, whatever seemed hopeless in my life was suffused with hope. Whatever despair I was experiencing over the suffering in the world now contained the seeds of glory. Even the sad, sad situation in the Middle East, which only seems to get worse, contained the possibility of new life. If only for a moment, that small Christian community of women gave me a glimpse of what eternity will be for all of us. For a few seconds I got it. I got why, for Paul, the suffering, the death, and the resurrection are all one for us. I felt strong and God's church felt strong.

Talking about What the Resurrection Means for Your Church

"So," writes Paul to the Corinthian church, "if anyone is in Christ, there is a new creation: everything old has passed away; see, everything has become new!" (II Corinthians 5:17).

Think about this passage for a few moments. You have been baptized in Christ. How do you experience this newness that Paul proclaims? It might be a transformation you have experienced in yourself or in someone who is close to you. It might be a kind of fresh vision of the world that you have been given through your life in Christ. Or maybe Paul's understanding that because of the resurrection of Christ, "…everything has become new!" is elusive for you in your personal life or your experience of the world. Perhaps, given the suffering in the lives of people around you and in the world, you don't see much reality in Paul's view of life. Spend some time talking about how you personally experience the resurrection of Jesus Christ.

Now shift the discussion to your congregation. In your life together as a church, how do your brothers and sisters in Christ receive this message of hope that we have because of the resurrection of Jesus Christ? Do members of your parish best hear God's word of hope through the preaching and teaching in your church, in their personal prayer, in corporate worship, or in serving others? Maybe you could spend a little of your discussion time evaluating how your Sunday or weekly worship reflects this sense of hopefulness that is so critical to Paul's understanding of God.

Like Paul, do you see your church as an agent of the resurrection in your local community or in the wider community of the world? If Christ's resurrection does mean the dawning of the new age, how does this influence the decisions you make as a vestry? How could discussing the ramifications of Paul's knowledge of the resurrection strengthen your life together? In what ways does it encourage you to take more risks?

As a vestry or in adult education class, talk about the implications of Paul's understanding of the resurrection given the state of the world today. As a believer in Jesus Christ, how do you make sense of the death and decay from war, poverty, and natural disasters? Where do you see signs in the world of the continual unfolding of God's glory in the risen Christ? What is specific to the lives of the people in your community that would make them doubt that the kingdom of God has come in the suffering, death, and resurrection of Jesus Christ?

For example, maybe you have a number of gay couples in your church. Given the slow acceptance of gay people in the church and the increased hostility across our country to equal rights for gay and lesbian people, do these couples see little to make them believe in the unfolding of the kingdom of God? Or, say you have several people in your congregation who are deeply concerned about the destruction of our environment. Given global warming and the unabated destruction of our environment, and the lack of concern by our federal and state governments, how do these people experience the promise of Christ's healing and restoring power through his death and resurrection? What do the members of racial or ethnic minorities in your congregation think of Paul's assertion of the unfolding of the kingdom of God?

Can you encourage your ordained and lay leadership to reflect in their preaching on the confusion you sometimes feel between what is reported in the news or what a marginalized person experiences and our Christian view of reality because of the resurrection? Can you encourage the editor of your newsletter to write of the pastoral implications of Paul's understanding of the resurrection for your parish and of the culture of negativity, which sometimes affects Christian community?

CHAPTER

FIVE

The Eucharist

M ANY SUNDAY evenings over the past few years, after I
have finished my visitation in a parish, I stop by to see
neighbors with a very active young family who live just
down the road from us. On these Sunday evenings, the two fathers
and I sit at their kitchen table, talking, interrupted by a constant
stream of requests, complaints, or questions from their four boys,
coming and going from another room. Often while we are sitting
at that kitchen table, talking about raising children, their marriage,
my life in community, our vocations, what the past week has been
like for each of us, and what we face in the week to come, I think
of a verse from an old Kate Wolf song: "Now it seems the truest
words I ever heard from you / Were said at kitchen tables we have
known / 'Cause somehow in that warm room, with coffee on the
stove / Our hearts were really most at home...."

For nine years I had the privilege of working with the first
woman bishop in the Anglican Communion, Barbara C. Harris. I
remember one occasion when she was planning a confirmation visitation with an affluent suburban parish in our diocese. The leadership of the parish informed Bishop Harris that following the service
of confirmation, there would be a luncheon for the young people
being confirmed and their families at the local country club, and they
hoped she would join them. She told them in that clear, direct way

of hers that she wouldn't be joining them at the country club, and she added a condition: if they wanted her to do the confirmation, then following the service, there would be a parish potluck, with everyone bringing a dish. Everyone in the congregation was to be included. Because Bishop Harris is an African American, and given the racist policies of most country clubs, one could easily understand her reluctance to celebrate a church sacrament at a country club.

But there was more to Bishop Harris's reaction than the experience of racism in exclusive clubs. She knows how important it is for people to cook for one another. She knows how eating together gathers a community. She knows that no matter how rich or poor the congregation, sharing a meal is critical to the health and vitality of a congregation. The experience of a meal prepared and shared by the whole community was the gift Bishop Harris wanted to give to those young people of privilege on their confirmation day.

All kinds of tables and meals are at the heart of the church. Perhaps this is what church members are communicating to me when a visitation potluck is over and someone almost always remarks, "One thing about our parish is, we sure love to eat." Potluck suppers, banquets, breakfast Bible study groups, guild luncheons, vestry meetings with supper, young people and pizza, fund-raising dinners, and Shrove Tuesday pancake suppers are all a kind of prayer for us. For like in prayer, at a meal, around a table, we seem to be more open to the presence of God. In the liturgy of preparing and setting out the meal, eating, and cleaning up, we become a kind of sacrament for one another. Like the Kate Wolf song says, at tables we seem to hear the truest words and have a sense that our hearts are most at home.

Letting Scripture Talk about the Eucharist

The meal, in almost any form, as a place to receive the revelation of God goes back to our earliest Christian ancestors in probably every decade, in every location around the Mediterranean, and from almost any theological perspective. When Matthew, Mark, Luke, and John want to speak the truest words concerning the identity of Jesus, to strengthen the fellowship, they do it through the sharing of a revealed in a meal. At breakfast on the beach of the Sea of Galilee, it is so obvious to the disciples that the Jesus who died on the cross is now alive and with them that they don't even question who he is as he prepares fish for them over an open fire (John 21:12).

The authors of the Gospels use the meal not only to reveal the identity of Jesus but as a forum for teaching and learning as well. Think of how often in Matthew, Mark, Luke, and John Jesus tells a story of a banquet to teach his disciples about God's forgiveness, about the celebration of his presence, or who will be invited into the kingdom of God (Luke 15:25–32; Mark 2:18–20; Matthew 22:1–14). Meals are also used by the writers of the Gospels to show Jesus' openness and availability to women. Except perhaps in the Roman aristocracy, a woman of their time would rarely have been invited to a meal with men. She might have been present serving the food but would not sit with the men and certainly would not anoint a man, as happens to Jesus in both Mark's and John's Gospels, just before he is put to death. "Leave her alone," says Jesus to those who are criticizing her presence (John 12:7 and Mark 12:7).

Used again and again as it is, the mention of a meal would have been like a magnet, drawing the attention of these early hearers of the Gospel, letting them know that something important is about to be said by God or about God. Is it any wonder, then, that the last meal Jesus shared with his followers had such significance for them? They would never forget the poignancy of this particular meal, taking place as it did around Passover, in an atmosphere of increasing fear of what would happen to Jesus and to themselves given the hostility of the religious authorities to his teaching and healing. You can imagine that his followers would never, ever be able to forget the deep sadness they felt at that meal and how paralyzed they must have felt about the danger they were certain was coming. After they witnessed Jesus' horrific suffering and death on the cross and experienced the inexplicable joy in his resurrection appearances, this last meal, with all of his words and actions, was sure to become part of their telling of the story.

The telling of that story might have gone something like this. Mary Magdalene, in her incredible joy on meeting in the garden her beloved teacher—not dead on the cross and lost to her forever, as she

meal. For example, the authors of all four Gospels use the miraculous feeding of the multitudes of four thousand or five thousand to
establish the identity of Jesus. Just think for a minute of how especially evocative a story of a meal provided by God for a multitude
in a deserted place would be for Jewish Christians in those first-
century house churches. All they would have to hear were the words
"hunger" and "wilderness" as the person telling the story during
their worship that day set the context for Jesus' feeding of four thousand or five thousand, and they would have been transported back
through the centuries, to when their starving ancestors were wan-
dering in the desert, from Egypt to the Promised Land. The Exodus
story of God providing manna for his people comes flooding back
into their consciousness. Now they are ready to hear of God's miraculous feeding of the multitudes through the hands of Jesus with just
five or seven loaves and a few small fish. Yes, this Jesus is indeed in
the tradition of the God of Israel (Mark 6:32–44 and 8:1–10;
Matthew 14:13–21 and 15:32–37; Luke 9:10–17; John 6:1–13).

When the author of Luke wanted to reveal to the community
of the church that Jesus has the power to forgive, a power that right-
fully belongs only to God, he did it through telling the poignant
story of the sinful woman. Uninvited, the woman enters the house
of Simon the Pharisee, where Jesus is dining. She weeps over his feet,
dries them with her hair, and anoints him with oil. Because the
woman is a sinner, Jesus' host, Simon, good Pharisee that he is, doubts
that Jesus could be the prophet some people have been saying that
he obviously is. Jesus proves he is a prophet and more. He tells Simon
he knows what he is thinking concerning this woman, through a
parable teaches his host the true nature of God's forgiveness, and then
forgives the woman, claiming God's power for himself (Luke
7:36–50). Like in the feeding of the multitudes, it is in a meal that
the true identity of Jesus is revealed to the gathered church.

The hearers of God's word in these first- and second-century
communities, from their familiarity with the ancient Hebrew stories
of God's revelation through a meal, and from what they have been
told of the revelation of who Jesus is through the stories of Gospel
meals, are more than ready now to hear of Christ's risen presence

thought, but alive and risen—went out from Jerusalem, maybe back to her village of Magdala, close to Capernaum on the Sea of Galilee. She went out boldly, and in gatherings of friends or strangers, to whoever would listen, she would tell her story of how her teacher, who had loved her and understood her more than anyone in the world, had suffered a horrible death but was now alive. She had seen him, he had spoken to her, and she had touched him. She must have recounted for her listeners not just what she saw from the foot of the cross or heard from the lips of his risen body in the garden, but also the final meal they had all shared on the night before his death: how Jesus gathered them all, what she felt as she looked into the faces of the family of his followers on that night, what they said to one another in quiet voices during the evening. Most likely, she wasn't actually at the table with the male disciples for their last supper together, but she may have been in the room, serving or watching in the background. In her reliving of that evening, she must have told those gathered around her in Magdala or some other village about how Jesus took the bread, blessed it, gave it to all the disciples, did the same with a cup of wine, and said, "Do this in remembrance of me" (I Corinthians 11:24).

Could it have been like that as well for Peter, Thomas, or James? Did they each go out with their own story about Jesus of Nazareth, who had cared for them, inspired them, given them a sense of their worth in God's eyes, forgiven them, died that awful, shameful death that made them so afraid, and then had come back to them, risen and alive? As they went out, did they, each in his own way, as they retold the whole story of those last days, remember as part of those last days that awful night, fraught with pain, and what Jesus did with the bread and the wine? Is that how they passed on the words they remembered Jesus saying: "Truly I tell you, I will never again drink of the fruit of the vine until that day when I drink it new in the kingdom of God" (Mark 14:25)? Did those first followers understand those words to mean that after his resurrection and ascension, Christ would be forever present to them in this meal? Did they believe, because of his words at the last meal they shared together, that in the celebration of this particular meal, they participated with him in the banquet of the kingdom of God?

And did that first generation keep retelling that story? Did they pray with it? Did they connect it with what they had read in the Hebrew scriptures and come to realize that every time they gathered for this meal, took the cup, broke the bread, and prayed the words, Christ was present with them, too, feeding them through the bread and wine and renewing them in hope for themselves and all creation through the suffering, death, and resurrection of Jesus Christ? Is that what the author of the Gospel of Luke is trying to communicate to his churches when he tells the story of the walk to Emmaus? Two disciples, you remember, walking along the road are joined by a mysterious stranger, who explains to them, by interpreting Hebrew scripture, all that they had experienced over the last few days in Jerusalem over the death of their friend. The three stop for a meal, and in the breaking of the bread, they recognize the stranger as Christ. "Were not our hearts burning within us," they say to each other after he has disappeared, "while he was talking to us on the road, while he was opening the scriptures to us?" (Luke 24:32–33). Is Luke portraying for his hearers through this story the rich experience of the next generation of followers and the one after that and the one after that? Is he directing his hearers to scripture and the meal for their experience of the resurrection?

It must have happened something like that, because that is just how Paul describes the meal and its meaning to the church in Corinth as little as twenty or twenty-five years after the death and resurrection of Jesus Christ (I Corinthians 11:23–26). In another instance of remarkable congruity, Matthew, Mark, and Luke say the same thing to their communities that Paul does to the Corinthians about this last meal Jesus shared with his disciples. These Gospels and Paul's letters all agree that in gathering to tell the story of Jesus' death and resurrection and in breaking the bread together and sharing the cup of wine, they experience Christ's presence until the final coming of the kingdom.

It looks as though each of these diverse first-century churches that we have been discussing, from as close to the beginning of their forming as we can imagine, celebrated this highly distinctive meal, which was, Paul says, "…received for the Lord" (I Corinthians 11:23).

Most likely, as in our churches today, many different kinds of meals were shared by members of house churches in Rome or Antioch or Corinth or wherever Jesus Christ was preached, but for the most part, like today, all those meals in all those congregations in all those different places potentially played some role in strengthening the members' life together in Christ. For in the partaking of this meal, the members entered the death and resurrection of Jesus Christ and experienced now the kingdom that was coming in its fullness. In partaking of the bread and wine, they were renewed through God's decisive act in history to make all things new in the offering of Jesus on the cross for our salvation and his victory over the grave. In eating this bread and drinking this cup with the gathered community, they entered the very core of God's revelation to us through Jesus Christ.

It isn't hard for us to imagine how much they needed this meal each week. Life must have been very hard for those first generations of Christians. Many of them were poor and had little influence in the vast Roman Empire. They were the kind of people who were most often the victims of decisions made in Rome about war or the distribution of grain or some new tax. They were the ones who lived in crowded, narrow alleys in major urban areas, with the constant fear of fire or quickly spreading disease. It must have been hard to get up in darkness to go to a long day of work and earn hardly enough to feed a family and still believe that through the death and resurrection of Jesus Christ, death and decay no longer ruled. Where was the evidence that "…all things work together for good…" (Romans 8:28)? How they must have longed each week to come together with their brothers and sisters to hear again the story of God's redemptive, final act in Jesus Christ; to praise God in song; to pray for one another; and then to break the bread and drink the wine, being fed and renewed in the risen presence of Christ.

Talking about What the Eucharist Means for Your Church

Spend some time talking about the meals your community shares together. Identify every meal for one another, from the Eucharist you share each week, the doughnuts at a weekday morning Bible study, and the Sunday coffee hour to the dinners celebrating important milestones in your church and the sandwiches you eat together at a stewardship meeting. What do you talk about at these meals? Can you remember a conversation at one of these meals that changed you in some way? An unexpected encounter with someone who said something that, on reflection, drew you deeper into the fellowship of the church and your relationship with God?

Now turn your discussion to the meal of the Eucharist. What is the experience of sharing this meal each week with the fellow members of your community like for you? In what ways do you experience the risen presence of Christ in the Eucharist? Do you usually experience the risen presence of Christ in the Eucharist as a feeling of hope or a sense of renewal, or perhaps something different? In reading scripture, in preaching, in prayer, or in receiving communion, have you ever been overwhelmingly certain of Christ's presence in the world and the unfolding of the kingdom of God? What role do the other members of your church play in your experience of the risen Christ in this meal? Or, to be honest, does the Eucharist hold a very small part in your relationship with God?

Throughout Christian history, church communities have discussed and sometimes altered how the community celebrates this meal so that it might draw the community into the deepest possible relationship with the risen Christ. For example, in the past thirty years, many denominations have radically altered their order of service in order to address the needs and context of their communities of faith. Many individual congregations explore new images for God in worship and adopt language that invites all of the people of God to the meal. As a spiritual leader of your parish, is this something you do? Why do you think people in your congregation regularly share in this meal? What parts of your weekly celebration of the Eucharist renew the faith life of your church? How are your fellow Christians challenged by this meal? What would you alter in your celebration of the Eucharist to strengthen your church?

CHAPTER

SIX

The Church

Letting Scripture Talk about the Church

The author of the Gospel of Matthew has the heart of a pastor. It is Matthew's concern for his people that undergirds all of his teaching, his dedication to continuity with the Law and the fulfillment of Hebrew scripture, and his attention to order and discipline. His concern was well placed: something was going terribly wrong with these churches in 85 CE in western Syria. Something was not working in Matthew's fellowship of believers.

Presumably, at one time there were people whose relationship with God had been dramatically changed through the telling of the story of Jesus Christ and their experience of his risen presence in the shared meal and in their fellowship with one another. These earlier generations must have felt changed, hopeful, and deeply connected to God through their life in this forming church. We can imagine that they must have been mostly Jewish men and women who had always been devout, but with this new presence of Christ in their lives, they must have felt that God had opened a whole new dimension of God's self to them. Presumably, there must have been enormous enthusiasm and energy in these earlier generations of the church, or they couldn't have survived the devastation of Jerusalem, the destruction of the Temple, and the pressure of the ruling religious authorities.

But not anymore. We can't be certain exactly what was going on outside their church that was affecting them so profoundly, but it was, apparently, something that previous generations had not had to face. Look at some of Jesus' sayings that Matthew chose and adapted from his sources to address his churches: "…you will be hated by all because of my name. But the one who endures to the end will be saved" (Matthew 10:22). And: "If another member of the church sins against you," Jesus says, "go and point out the fault when the two of you are alone. If the member listens to you, you have regained that one. But if you are not listened to, take one or two others along with you, so that every word may be confirmed by the evidence of two or three witnesses. If the member refuses to listen to them, tell it to the church" (Matthew 18:15–17). That sounds like a pretty serious threat from outside the congregation and substantive disagreement going on in the church.

It might have gone something like this: Perhaps the conviction of these former Jews that Jesus was the longed-for messiah was threatening to their Jewish neighbors. Matthew's community might have been experiencing some kind of harassment or even violence from these Jewish neighbors. That shouldn't surprise us. It is a fairly normal occurrence for a forming religious group to experience opposition from the group of which it was formerly a part. If this was the kind of opposition they were experiencing, it would make sense that there would be internal dissension and confusion. Maybe, for example, there were members of Matthew's churches who were stunned by the opposition they were experiencing from former friends or relatives. Perhaps they questioned their own commitment to Christ as a consequence. It isn't too hard for us to imagine that there would be one or two members, or a group of members, saying to their church, "Look, maybe our opponents are right. Maybe we should be listening to them." Perhaps you can recall something like this happening to you when you felt called to make a significant change in your life that challenged the beliefs or values of the people you love. It is hard to stand up to that kind of opposition.

Positions within the community seem to have hardened. You know from your experience in a community what happens in a situation like this. People are so certain they are right that they stop engaging one another. What is fatal is that they often assume that God is on their side, and so they also stop engaging God. Under these circumstances, how could God possibly tell them anything new? How do you effect the compromise so necessary to any kind of community life? No wonder Matthew addresses his churches with this saying of Jesus: "They were harassed and helpless, like sheep without a shepherd" (Matthew 9:36). Who would want to be a leader in a situation like this? Think how hard it would be to bring about reconciliation and provide a vision of a hopeful future for a community that is divided into factions.

What do you do when a once-vibrant church is floundering like this? How do you build up the congregation and make it strong again?

Matthew's answer was to write a Gospel that would speak directly to the situation of his community. Matthew's congregations had probably already been hearing in their weekly worship for as many as twenty or thirty years portions of the Gospel that Mark had written to his churches in Antioch. They most likely had other written texts that contained the preaching of Jesus during his public ministry, texts that must have been incorporated into their regular gatherings as well. And, of course, these little congregations must have had their own cherished stories of Jesus of Nazareth that had been told to them by their founder and passed down through the generations.

But, for some reason, the congregations of Matthew either weren't listening to any of this or it wasn't providing the renewal and vision that it had in the past. It didn't quite fit the bill. Matthew knew that for these little churches to remain vibrant they needed more teaching. So he took everything he knew about what Jesus had taught and shaped it and edited it in a way that would make the community strong and able to stand up to the external stresses that were so disorienting for them.

For example, Matthew knew how critical corporate and individual prayer was to the faith life of these communities. He knew that unless the individuals in these churches were taking responsibility for their relationships with God through prayer, they would never be able to do God's work together creatively. Perhaps some of the members of Matthew's communities were enamored of the kind of prayer that is mostly outward show (Matthew 6:5). He knew this ostentatious kind of prayer was not about communicating with God and only served to increase the self-righteousness of the one who was praying like this and to further divide the community. Instead, Matthew offers his churches Jesus' simple but profound prayer as a way of connecting with God (Matthew 6:9–13). Prayer, if it was going to strengthen the church, should show humility, forgiveness, and dependence, and be intimate and from the heart.

Matthew also knew how important almsgiving could be to the deepening of a person's relationship with God. Generosity is a hall-mark of the nature of God, and so if we are made in God's image and likeness, then we are most ourselves when we are generous to others. For certain, Matthew wanted the people of his churches to give money to provide care for others and for the spread of the gospel of Christ, but he also wanted his people to know that giving had great potential for enhancing their relationship with God and with one another. Yet, with ostentatious prayer, he knew that exces-sive public displays of almsgiving were likely to cause envy and sus-picion in a community. Matthew offers this to his community from the teachings of Jesus: "But when you give alms, do not let your left hand know what your right hand is doing, so that your alms may be done in secret; and your Father who sees in secret will reward you" (Matthew 6:3–4). Like prayer and fasting, if it is to strengthen the life of the community and draw a person deeper into their relation-ship with God, almsgiving is best done in secret to insure humility and dependence on God rather than reputation. "Beware" says Jesus, "of practicing your piety before others in order to be seen by them" (Matthew 6:1).

Matthew cautions the people of his churches against judging one another (Matthew 7:1). He knows how destructive grudges can be and how important forgiveness is if men and women are to wor-ship and work together for God's kingdom. So he tells the wonder-ful story of Peter asking Jesus how often he should forgive someone in the church who sins against him. Knowing that misunderstandings and hurting one another are inevitable in any group of people, Jesus tells Peter that to have a strong church, you have to forgive infinite times (Matthew 18:21–22). Like this example, Jesus' teaching, parables, and the stories of his ministry in the Gospel of Matthew are always about justice, mercy, and trust—precisely those attributes that increase the health and vitality of the congregation.

To strengthen this community, Matthew reminds it again and again of its lineage. Through his repeated use of Hebrew scripture quotations, he reminds his people that Jesus of Nazareth is the Messiah for whom the Jewish people long. Right from the lengthy list of Jesus' ancestors in the first chapter of the Gospel through to his evocative use of phrases from the psalms in his account of the suffering and death of Jesus in the twenty-seventh chapter, Matthew wants the members of his church always to be aware of who Jesus of Nazareth is. You will remember from chapter two that he goes to great lengths to prove over and over again that Jesus of Nazareth is not the founder of some new religion but the fulfillment of all that has gone before in Judaism. "Do not think," says the Jesus of Matthew, "that I have come to abolish the law or the prophets; I have come not to abolish but to fulfill" (Matthew 5:17).

Matthew wasn't interested in merely mending fences within the church and establishing a unity to help the members of his church withstand whatever opposition they were facing from the outside. He wanted growth. He wanted trained missionaries who could go out and found new churches. He knew that if a community isn't emphasizing and working for growth in membership, it will shrink and eventually die. By recalling Jesus' missionary instructions and the sending out of his twelve disciples, Matthew gives the people of his church very specific information about how they are to do this critical work (Matthew 10:5).

Not too many years ago, an old, much-revered, and deeply loved member of our monastic community died. We celebrated his long life with great gratitude, and we put a photograph of him on the wall of our common room, next to one of another beloved member of the community who had died. He hadn't always been held in high esteem in the fellowship of the community. In fact, at one time his reputation was that of a cantankerous gossip who was stifling the growth of our community and could be quite hurtful to people.

Then he changed. I wondered: How, in the space of a few years, did he go from being this hard-hearted, close-minded person to being this amusing, compassionate, even visionary old man? I lived side by side with him for more than twenty years, and as far as I know, there was no significant event or relationship that would have caused this radical transformation. He seemed to continue doing what he had always done in terms of his Christian practice.

All the puzzling I have done over his transformation has led me to one conclusion. He changed because his life in the community changed him. Years of disagreements, praying, fasting, being forgiven, hurt, compassion, and ministry—everything that makes up the community of the church—worked on him. I don't think he made any special effort during the last few years of his life. I am sure the other members of the fellowship of the church didn't try harder to incorporate him or make him feel more loved. I am ashamed to say that I didn't reach out to him in any special way. I think it was just the structure of our community, how we agreed to live together in Christ through our rule and our life together, that changed him and probably changed us in our living with him as well. I believe that is how grace came to him and to us and how he came to die as one who was visibly made in the image and likeness of God.

I think this is what Matthew had in mind in his Gospel. He wanted to set up a community, a church, that would change people. He provided rules about praying, forgiving, giving of resources, and almost every aspect of life together. Then he said: Put yourself in the middle of this, be committed to this for the whole rest of your life, and it will change you.

Matthew knew a lot about the way grace works. He knew that many of these third-generation Christians in his churches were probably not going to have a single, powerful life-changing encounter with the risen Christ. He knew enough about human nature to know that most people aren't going to turn their lives around just by their own effort. He knew that most of us are brought into the fullness of who we are in the Kingdom of God slowly, almost imperceptibly, over a lifetime of living in a community infused with the presence of Christ. He wanted a strong, vibrant community because he knew of its converting power. This is why I believe Matthew had the heart of a pastor and cared so deeply for the lost and harassed of his community. This is why his writings were called a Gospel and handed down to all the churches for all time. Matthew had my old brother in mind.

Talking about What the Church Means for Your Church

Of course, our situation in the twenty-first century is not exactly like the situation of Matthew's churches in the first century. Nonetheless, begin your discussion on the church by thinking with one another about the challenges the church faces from the outside.

Start with Christianity as a whole, and share where you believe Christianity faces its greatest opposition. Do you think, for example, that secularism or consumerism is the biggest threat Christianity faces in North American culture? Is a plurality of other faiths an opposing force to ours? Or something else?

Now shift your discussion to our denomination, the Episcopal Church and the Anglican Communion. What opposition are we enduring right now from outside of ourselves? Is it conflicting worldviews between continents that is threatening the unity of our Anglican family? What about the local level, your diocese or your local church community? Where and how are you being challenged from the outside?

Can you identify, as Matthew did for his churches, how this opposition from the outside has caused internal stress or even conflict in the church community, especially in your congregation? What are some of the manifestations of the stress in your church? Matthew seems to draw on particular teachings of Jesus that he believes will help his brothers and sisters in Christ grow through the stress and become a stronger community in order to witness effectively to the power of God through Jesus Christ in the world.

Knowing as you do the people for whom you provide leadership, and given the particular stress or conflict you face in your congregation, what teachings of Jesus would you choose to build yours into a healthy church?

Matthew believed that Jesus' teachings on prayer, forgiveness, evangelism and mission, the sharing of resources, the development of leadership, and the use and study of scripture were all extremely important to the vibrancy of the community of the church. How do you, as the spiritual leaders of your church, invite your people into a richer experience of prayer or a sense of God's forgiveness? How are you developing future leaders for your congregation? What qualities do you look for in lay leaders for your parish? How do you share the leadership gifts you have to strengthen the larger church?

Finally, Matthew actually taught the people of his communities through his Gospel how to go out and tell the world of Jesus Christ and bring new people into the fellowship. How do you prepare your people to do this kind of work?

CHAPTER SEVEN

Stewardship, Budgets, and Capital Campaigns

TWELVE YEARS ago, as a very new bishop, I had an experiment I wanted to try. In order for me to learn about the parishes of the diocese, I wanted my visitations to last a whole day so I could meet with all the various groups of the church and have time to listen to the whole congregation. This meant that some parish visits would have to be made on Saturdays. I was a little nervous and uncertain about how the clergy would respond to my innovation, so I decided I would try out my idea with a representative number of clergy and get their impressions. Of the many pastoral visits I made when I first became bishop, I remember one to a seasoned rector of a large suburban parish. I could tell from the moment we sat down together that he was not in a very receptive mood. He had just come from a long, frustrating budget meeting with the vestry of the church. The bottom line of their discussion, he told me, was there simply wasn't enough pledged income to cover expenses.

"Tom," he said to me, "these are good, generous people. When they say to me they have yearly financial commitments to causes such as cancer research, conservation and the Audubon Society, their colleges, and local arts programs, and that they simply can't pledge any more to cover the care of our buildings, staff salaries, the outreach of the church, and our assessment to the diocese, how can I argue with them?"

"Oh," I wanted to say to him but only thought to myself, "let me at them! I'll tell them their giving to the church isn't about buildings, salaries, and perpetuating a worthy institution. It's about their spiritual transformation. What they give has to do with living the life of the resurrection." I went on in my mind. "Let me talk to them. I'll tell them that as important as their donations are to these nonprofits, their pledge to the church is about more than the ministry they make possible. Their pledge is about expressing our unity in Christ; it is about the reality of the kingdom of God. I'll have no problem telling them why they should increase their pledges. The gift of money is, after all, an act of prayer."

But, as I said, I was a new bishop and maybe a little timid, so I didn't say any of this. Now, thirteen years later, I can try to say why money and the giving of money to the church are so important to us as Christian men and women, through examining some of Paul's letters and his appeals for money from those struggling, mostly poor, little communities he founded and served across the Mediterranean world.

Letting Scripture Talk about Money

Paul spent a fair amount of his time talking about money. He wrote to the congregations in Galatia how pleased he was to collect money for the church in Jerusalem (Galatians 2:10). Paul gave instructions to the people in Corinth on how, each week, they were to put aside something of what they earned for the benefit of the church (I Corinthians 16:1–4). He told the congregations in Rome that the collection from the communities for which he was responsible was so important that it had actually kept him from visiting them and pursuing his mission work in Spain (Romans 15:27–28). Paul was grateful to the Philippians for all the support they gave to him (Philippians 4:15–18).

What is it about giving money to the church that is so important to Paul? It wasn't for the usual reasons, the kind we hear about in modern stewardship appeals. He wasn't asking for money for buildings or salaries or even programs. While Paul most likely had great compassion for the poor in Jerusalem, it is obvious from reading his letters that he is eager to collect this money for a reason even greater than providing food and shelter for the indigent. For Paul, giving money was directly related to his understanding of what it is to be a human being in Christ; I don't think I am putting words in Paul's mouth when I say that for him, giving money was a concrete affirmation of a first-century Christian's belief in the resurrection. Money is deeply theological for Paul. What he wrote about money had everything to do with building up the faith life of his congregations.

Let me see if I can get at what I think Paul is saying about money by talking about sex. Do you remember how angry Paul is with his brothers and sisters in Christ in the little house churches in Corinth because he has heard that they are condoning sexual immorality (I Corinthians 5 & 6)? We can't be certain why these Christian men and women were putting up with this kind of behavior in their community any more than we can be entirely certain why Paul feels he has to speak out so strongly against fornication. It might have been that there were some members of the congregation who mistakenly believed that because they were in Christ and because the coming of the kingdom was imminent, they didn't have to worry about their behavior. It could have been that an influential part of this forming Christian community mistakenly believed that their new life in the Spirit gave them complete license to do as they pleased in their lives. They might have thought that only their worship and their prayer, their miracles, and speaking in tongues were important to God and the ministry and worship of the church.

That isn't what Paul is thinking. He isn't being a prude about sex in his first letter to the Corinthians. He is making an important point about the resurrection of Jesus Christ. Throughout this long letter, Paul is saying, in various ways, Look, because Christ has been raised from the dead, everything has been transformed. The whole of life has been caught up in the Spirit, including your body. Your body matters. In fact, he says, "…Do you not know that your body is a temple of the Holy Spirit within you…?" (I Corinthians 6:19). Because of Christ's resurrection, the rest of your life can't be compartmentalized from you spiritual life with God. Even your flesh is caught up in the life of the Spirit.

Paul's understanding of the resurrection embraces the whole of who we are: our bodies, our relationships, what we do to earn a living, and even how we spend our wages. Every part of a person's life is an avenue into a deeper experience of God through the resurrection of Jesus Christ. Money becomes not something we simply save, spend on food and clothing, use to provide for our families, or use to buy luxuries for ourselves; like everything of the material world, it participates in God's victory through Jesus Christ.

As Paul tries to get us to look at the cosmic implications of the resurrection in our lives, he comes at it from the other side as well. You can't compartmentalize your spiritual life, either, he reminds us. You know those spiritual gifts you have been given of which you are so proud, he writes to the Corinthians, like prophecy, speaking in tongues, or the working of miracles. You can't isolate those any more than you can isolate your own body from life in the Spirit. You can't think that you are a very spiritual person just because you speak in tongues. No, all these spiritual gifts are meant for something concrete. "To each," he writes, "is given the manifestation of the Spirit for the common good" (I Corinthians 12:7). All those pieces that seem so unconnected in our lives—sex, how we relate to one another, what we do, what we think, what we eat, and also our spiritual gifts—because of Christ's resurrection, are deeply connected. It's what Paul means when he says that in Christ we are made whole.

So our money has to be part of the resurrection, too. What is the role of money in the resurrection experience for Paul? My bet is that Paul knew as much about how separated people were from one another as anybody could in the first century. After all, he traveled a lot. He saw firsthand how many different languages were spoken in the Roman Empire, how wide the gap was between rich and poor, how different the values were in Macedonia from those on the island of Crete, and how the multitude of religions across the

Mediterranean world separated people. He heard the grumbling about oppressive taxes, civil uprisings, and wars.

Paul writes to the church in Galatia, "They asked only one thing, that we remember the poor, which is exactly what I was eager to do" (Galatians 2:10). Paul is writing here to the mostly Gentile believers in Jesus Christ in Galatia about a request he received at his meeting with the mostly Jewish believers in Jesus Christ in Jerusalem around 50 CE. He is relating to the churches he founded in what is now western Turkey how, at this critical meeting in Jerusalem, it was recognized by the whole church there that he "...had been entrusted with the gospel for the uncircumcised, just as Peter had been entrusted with the gospel for the circumcised..." (Galatians 2:7). That church agreed that the Gentile believers in Jesus Christ with whom Paul was having so much success did not have to live under the Law and were not required to be circumcised or to follow the dietary rules the Jewish believers in Jesus Christ were encouraged to follow.

Both sides seemed to have agreed to forming a way of life together in Christ that would embrace different theologies, different missionary ventures, different ways of organizing local churches, and different lifestyles appropriate to the various cultures of the Roman Empire. But what every church had to do, regardless of its culture or what its members believed or how it was configured, was give to the poor in Jerusalem. In spite of all the differences and disagreements across the churches, this giving of financial support to the church in Jerusalem for the caring of the poor, those he refers to as the saints, was the one thing Paul required them to do. He went to a great deal of trouble to make sure this support was provided. The collection for the poor in Jerusalem is referred to in his letter to the Romans, both of his letters to the Corinthians, his letter to the church in Philippi, and his letter to the churches in Galatia. From his extensive ministry in such a variety of places, Paul knew how separated all these different churches were from one another. He knew how different Jewish believers in Christ were from Gentile believers in Christ. Because Paul was a Pharisee, he was keenly aware of how different one Jew could be from another. It is pretty clear from his letters that he understood how disconnected people could be from one another, even within the house churches to which he preached and for whom he cared.

But Paul also knew of God's longing for all people to be one. It is something he would have read about in Hebrew scripture, from prophets like Isaiah. "Nations shall come to your light, and kings to the brightness of your dawn. Lift up your eyes and look around; they all gather together, they come to you" (Isaiah 60:3–4). Paul knew that God has enabled this longed-for unity through the death and resurrection of Jesus Christ. Money was a concrete expression of that unity. I would say the giving of money was almost a sacrament for him. That's why Paul cared so much about that Jerusalem collection. That's why he pleaded for money in his letters and, at considerable danger to himself, delivered the money to Jerusalem. The giving of money was the declaration that an individual donor or a struggling little church in some place like Thessaloniki believed that no matter what separates us in the world, through the resurrection of Christ, we are one.

Here's an example. She had what some Africans call a "traditional build" and a smile as big as God's heart. Even before I got out of the Land Rover, I could feel her energy and presence across the churchyard as she stood there, with her arms spread wide enough to embrace the seven of us from the Diocese of Massachusetts at once. Marching back and forth all around us were boy scouts, girl scouts, and children in school uniforms, bearing banners of welcome and chanting, "Maggie Geller, you are my lover. Elisabeth Keller, you are my lover. Tom Shaw, you are my lover."

We were in Kenya, visiting the first of four churches that day. The young people and children marching and singing our praises were some of the 3,500 kids orphaned by HIV/AIDS for whom our diocese provides the funds for food, medical care, and teaching each week. The woman with the smile and the outstretched arms was Trophina, the founder, organizer, and driving force behind the men and women of these four Anglican churches who volunteer every Saturday to teach and prepare the food for the orphans. Five years before this visit, our diocese had voted to give 0.7% of our budget each year to support HIV/AIDS programs in Africa, and this was one of our first. You can imagine how, all at once, as we emerged from our vehicle, we felt overwhelmed by the enormity of the suffering before us and how we felt gratitude to God for leading our diocese to these courageous and dedicated people.

The Diocese of Maseno North, where Trophina and her fellow lay volunteers carry out their ministry to the orphans, not far from Lake Victoria, in western Kenya, is a long way from the Diocese of Massachusetts in the United States. The two dioceses are far apart not only in miles but in material resources and theology as well. Most in the Anglican Communion would consider our diocese wealthy and the Kenyan diocese very poor. Most would characterize us, like many of the dioceses of the Episcopal Church in the United States, as a liberal diocese, and Maseno North, like much of the rest of the Anglican Church in Kenya, as conservative and evangelical.

I think of Paul and his understanding of money when I write of my friend Trophina in the Anglican Diocese of Maseno North in Kenya and the Episcopal Diocese of Massachusetts in the United States. There is so much that separates us. Yet in our giving of this money and in her receiving this money from us for her critical ministry, our unity in Christ becomes a reality for all of us. It's the same, I think, in parishes, in dioceses, and in provinces of the church. There is so much that separates individuals in a parish, so much that separates the parishes of a diocese, the dioceses of a province: class, skin color, gender, education, age, theology; and yet, in our giving of our money, we declare that all the walls that separate us are broken down through the resurrection of Jesus Christ. We are one in Christ.

When I was a boy, our parish priest introduced incense for the first time at the celebration of the Eucharist one Christmas Eve. The layman who was responsible for rehearsing those of us who were to be acolytes on that night prepared us for this innovation in our worship by telling us that incense, with its rising smoke and sweet-smelling odor, was a kind of symbol of our prayers going up to heaven. I now appreciate the use of incense, because it involves the sense of smell, along with touch and our other senses, as a way of including the whole of who we are in our praise of God. But way back then, as a boy, drawn to mystery and the transcendent, I loved our acolyte director's explanation of the rising smoke of incense as a symbol of my prayers going up to God.

Paul writes to his brothers and sisters in Christ in the congregation in Philippi, "…Now that I have received from Epaphroditus the gifts you sent, a fragrant offering, a sacrifice acceptable and pleasing to God" (Philippians 4:18). The gifts he is referring to in this passage are of money from the church in Philippi to help Paul, who, it appears, is in prison in Ephesus. Unlike other references to money in his letters, this one is a reference not to the collection for the poor in Jerusalem but to an offering from his fellow believers in Christ made directly to Paul, whom they love and appreciate for all that he has done for them, in recognition of his terrible situation.

While Paul is moved by the generosity of the Philippian fellowship, he sees their offering as more than a gift to him. As my acolyte director likened incense smoke to prayer rising to heaven, Paul uses the language of worship to describe this very practical gift of money, and by doing so, he says that it is more than something practical to alleviate his sufferings; because it is a "fragrant offering," a "sacrifice acceptable and pleasing to God," it is prayer to him. Money, given by the people of God to the church, is prayer.

Paul is telling me by way of those Philippian Christians that giving money to the church is not only a demonstration of our unity in Christ, but it is prayer, like the intercessions I make each morning, like the psalms I pray in Morning and Evening Prayer, and like the grace I say before each meal. What we give to the life of the church is much, much more than support for budgets, the increase in the salary of the parish administrator, or the maintenance of buildings. It is a way of communicating with God. It is part of how we express the mystery of our relationship to our creator. The offering of money, instead of being simply the practical support of the church, is recognition on our part of the transcendent nature of God and God's sovereignty over all of creation.

Finally, giving money to the church in Jerusalem was a kind of statement of hope that in Jesus Christ, the kingdom of God had begun. As a Jew who had prayed with Hebrew scripture the whole of his life, Paul knew from Isaiah that the restoration of Jerusalem was the sign of God's coming. The restoration of Jerusalem would begin with the relief of the oppressed, the binding of the broken-hearted, and the release of captives (Isaiah 61:1). It is almost impossible for us to comprehend how bold it was for them to make this statement of hope.

You might get a glimmer of their boldness if you look at it in this way. Even in the relatively secure environment of a Western nation in the twenty-first century, you have probably felt from time to time at the mercy of events or people outside of your control. Recall the anger and frustration and hopelessness you felt. At your lowest ebb, you might well have thought, "What is the point of even trying when some other person or event will actually dictate the final outcome of my situation?"

That is probably how most of the people who lived in Paul's first-century world felt every day of their lives. The people to whom Paul ministered were like the vast majority of the people of the Roman Empire: slaves, poor people, and artisans, those who had little influence in the world. They were the kind of people who were at the mercy of drought in a distant land, which would determine their food supply. These people had no resources against plague, urban fires, war, or the capricious decisions of the government in Rome. But because of Jesus of Nazareth, his life, death, and resurrection, they knew that God had initiated the release of captives, the binding up of those who were brokenhearted, and the salvation of all who were oppressed. God was in charge of the whole of creation (Romans 8:38–39). Because of Christ, they were no longer victims, but actually participants in the coming of a new kingdom.

Giving money for the spread of this good news of Jesus Christ was a kind of concrete affirmation of the hope they now had for the world, the supreme statement of confidence that God's kingdom was unfolding before their eyes. For, surely, these early Christians could have given just to the poor in their own cities or in their own regions. Poverty, widows, orphans, the hungry were present everywhere. Why should the people of the little towns in Galatia give to people they would never meet, people living hundreds of miles from them, in Jerusalem? Why should Paul risk his life on bandit-infested roads and storm-tossed seas to get to Jerusalem with the money collected from places like Corinth, Thessalonica, or Philippi? Given all of Paul's differences with the church in Jerusalem and the way he had been treated by it, why did he even care? For these early Christians, placing their money on Jerusalem was placing their lives on the truth that God's victory through Jesus Christ had begun on Golgotha and in the empty tomb. In Hebrew scripture, it was a well-developed notion that God's restoration and the enactment of justice would begin in God's return to Jerusalem as the focal point of the whole world. Because this expectation was in place, Paul and these early Jewish followers of Christ would have made the connection between God's return and the return of Jesus. To have the poor set free from want in Jerusalem would show the world of the coming of the kingdom. Investing in Jerusalem not only tied them to God's redemptive acts through his chosen people but also bound the whole world to the fulfillment of God's kingdom in Jesus Christ.

Talking about What Money Means for Your Church

Paul believed that an offering of money to the church in Jerusalem was an expression of our unity in Christ, a prayer we offer to God, and a concrete declaration of our hope for the world through the good news of Jesus Christ. He doesn't seem to have been shy about asking for money or discussing it with the people he was forming in Christ. However, in many of the visits I make to parishes, money is one of the hardest subjects to talk about. Why do you think it is so difficult for us to talk about money and giving to the church? Have you increased your pledge over the past five years? If you have, what was it that made you want to give more? Did you hear a stewardship sermon, read something in your parish newsletter, or hear an effective talk by a member of the stewardship committee? Is that what impressed you?

Do you pray for an increase in giving in the prayers of the people at the Sunday Eucharist? When you have a difficult decision around the budget in a vestry meeting, do you ever stop the discussion and pray together? Have you ever thought of your giving as a kind of prayer, as Paul suggests?

When was the last time you, as a leader in your congregation, paused for a moment and thought about what your financial pledge accomplishes in proclaiming the kingdom of God? For example, consider the healing your faith community offers to people; the hope or peace your weekly worship brings to the men, women, and children in your parish; and the witness you make to the world about Sabbath time. Your money is incredibly important to the lives of many. Do you ever, in your prayer, let God thank you for the money you offer to the church?

In many denominations, as we do in the Episcopal Church, a parish is asked to pledge part of its budget to a larger body, like a diocese or regional church. Do you see this primarily as a kind of "tax"? Do you ever think of that gift to the larger church as a sign of our unity in Christ? How do we express our unity?

What do you think parishioners today want to hear from the church about giving money? As a leader of your church, how are you inviting them into the stewardship of their resources?

EIGHT

❖

Conflict

T HIS CHAPTER is not meant to solve any of our many conflicts in the twenty-first-century church. It is not a chapter about human sexuality, equality in the roles of women, biblical literalism, or even how scripture might inform our discussions around some of these important contemporary issues. It is not a chapter that will lead your congregation to a conflict-free future, and I won't offer you in this chapter any advice on the role of consultants in parish conflicts. I won't tell you when it is best to avoid conflict, engage it, or just try to live with it. I can't promise you a future in your church where people's feelings won't get hurt, where grudges won't be held for decades, or where people won't leave the church, taking their considerable financial support with them. Because, the fact is, no matter how kind and well meaning we Christians are, there is going to be conflict in Christian community.

More than three decades ago, I joined the monastic community of which I am still a member. I sometimes describe the day I was received into the community as a kind of coming home for me. For in the monastic life, and specifically in my community, with its strong emphasis on contemplative prayer and active ministry, I felt I had finally found the place where I belonged.

I took to this new life like a duck to water. I loved praying the offices, studying, and the companionship of most of my brothers, and I threw myself into almost any job I was given. And yet, in many ways, those early years of my vocation were some of the angriest and unhappiest in my life. Back then, and to a lesser degree even now, thirty years on, I often found myself internally and also externally in deep conflict with one or more of my brothers.

How could it be any different? When you join a community, whether it is a monastic community like mine or a parish like yours, you open yourself to the existence of others. You expose yourself to the needs and assumptions of other people, who most likely have very different backgrounds and desires from your own.

Letting Scripture Talk about Conflict

Think of the people the author of Mark brought together in those house churches in Antioch. He was exposing Jewish believers in Christ to Gentile followers of Jesus. Men were meeting women in worship. The people who knew Jesus as a healer were being exposed to those who knew Jesus as the apocalyptic preacher. Those who needed to know Jesus as their wise teacher were meeting those who treasured Jesus as the one who had suffered and died on the cross.

Maybe among them was an older Jewish man displaced from the Galilee. Imagine him as a deeply religious man who cherished the ancient covenant between God and his chosen people. Think of him as a man whose whole life was saturated with the Hebrew scripture and who longed for the day when his people would be free from their Roman oppressors. You can see how he might be attracted to the apocalyptic preacher Jesus of Nazareth and might recognize him as the Messiah. As good and kind a man as he might have been, you can understand how the traditions of his religion and culture, how the religious and civil code of his day, which viewed women as property of their fathers and husbands, influenced him to treat women the way he probably did. He wasn't abusive to them. But given who he was, it would have been almost impossible for him to imagine sharing a meal, sitting at the same table, with a woman of his own faith, let alone a Gentile.

Think about her. She is another displaced person. She isn't from the Galilee. She is from the coast and farther to the north. Like most people in the first century, she is deeply religious, but she isn't Jewish. This woman came to Antioch because her husband died. The law didn't allow her to inherit her husband's small plot of land. It went to his brother, who, because of the burden of the Roman taxes, couldn't afford to care for her and her children as well as his own family. So she left with her children for Antioch, where she thought she might find work. Together, they lived in a crowded alleyway. When her daughter got so sick, some people who believed in a healer called Jesus brought food for her family and prayed over her daughter in the name of this Jesus. And her daughter got well. The woman loved the way these people cared for her and others. It didn't seem to matter who it was, poor, Gentile, woman, child, these followers of Jesus cared for them. It was because of this care that she went to their meetings, that she listened to all the stories of how Jesus of Nazareth healed and how his Spirit was with this group now. She prayed with them, and they invited her to share the meal with them.

Now picture this. One week the woman, the Gentile from the coast, who has heard of these other followers of Jesus halfway across the city, the group to which the older devout Jewish man from the Galilee belongs, decides to visit them and share in their meal. Imagine, given who he was and who she had become, the explosion that might have taken place when she walked in the door of their house church, expecting to share in their meal. Imagine the accusations he might have made. Imagine, given all she had been through and all she had been given by her community, how she might have stood up to him. Imagine the divided loyalties in both communities, the sides people might have taken, after the event had taken place and the news got back to her own congregation.

This could not have been an easy conflict for these communities to resolve. There was so much at stake on both sides, so much that was precious to so many different people, so much each of the churches might lose. I wouldn't be surprised if there were threats, departures, letters written, and sermons preached before the dust had settled and a new church was born, one that wrapped its huge arms around everyone; male and female, Jew and Gentile.

I think that might have been the story behind the story that Mark tells of Jesus and the Gentile Syrophoenician woman in the Tyre region. It is always the task of narrative to tidy things up, and that is, I think, what the author of Mark does in this story (Mark 7:24–30). I think, in the telling of this story, he offers us a wonderful, miraculous conclusion to a long and sometimes bitter debate.

Most likely, every time we encounter requests, questions, and answers in the Gospel of Mark, they reflect a conflict in these house churches in Antioch. Does the request of James and John to sit on the right hand and the left hand of Jesus when he comes into his glory represent a hotly contested bid for leadership of these early communities (Mark 10:35–40)? Given that there doesn't appear to be any clearly defined lay or ordained leadership this early on in the church, how could there not have been disputes about who should be responsible for leading these little house churches? Given the models of leadership they had experienced in civil society and in their religious associations, be it Jewish or Gentile, how could there not have been debates over how leadership would be exercised in this newly forming church? Of course, if the intention of Mark was to draw these disparate house churches together, he would reach back into the sayings or teachings of Jesus that had been passed down to him in an effort to resolve the inevitable conflict over leadership in these congregations. Think what it must have been like for all of them when, after all their wrangling over who would be in charge, they could actually hear this story of a leadership of self-sacrifice, humility, and service.

It is apparent in all four Gospels that John the Baptist had a large group of followers. No matter how well intentioned were the disciples of John and the disciples of Jesus, there would have been competition between the two groups. Both of these men were popular and charismatic, and they obviously had profound faith in God. Just as Jesus' powerful teaching, his preaching, and the memory of his miracles lived on after him, there is every reason to believe that after John the Baptist's death, his followers continued to preach his message of repentance. The conflict between the two groups, no doubt, would have been handed down to future generations of their respective followers. It is more than likely that the next generation of their disciples would have had debates when they met one another in Antioch in the late 60s. Mark's retrieval of the exchange between Jesus and his disciples at Caesarea Philippi from the stories of Jesus handed down to him could well have been an effort to bring closure to these perhaps bitterly divided loyalties (Mark 8:27–30).

From the conflicts that must have racked those forming churches for which Mark wrote his Gospel comes a new vision for the community of God. From the conflicts emerges a new kind of leadership, one that embraces suffering and serving for the sake of the life of the community. From all the disagreement, hurt feelings, and misunderstanding comes a church with a table so expansive that everyone is seated together, and all share in the common meal. From all the passion spent by the rivalry between the disciples of John the Baptist and Jesus of Nazareth comes the clear identity of the Messiah.

Unlike in the tidy narrative of Mark, there is nothing to mask the conflict going on in the congregations of Paul. From Paul's letters to the churches in Corinth, Rome, Galatia, and Philippi, and even to his beloved church in Thessalonica, it is apparent that at one time or another, they were all racked with controversy. Sometimes the contention was caused by different factions within the congregation; sometimes the controversy was between Paul and the local church; at other times the conflict was caused by interlopers who taught doctrines contrary to the witness of Paul.

For example, there is every reason to believe that Paul's most highly developed theology and exquisitely crafted letter written to the churches in Rome was actually born in conflict. Paul's letter to the Romans, probably the last of his letters that we have, appears to have been written to Gentile believers in Christ who were being dismissive of God's revelation in the Judaism of their Jewish Christian brothers and sisters. These Gentile Christians seem to have forgotten their roots.

At the time Paul wrote this letter, in the late 50s, there were maybe a dozen house churches in Rome, some of which apparently barely knew of the existence of the others. Before this letter was written, Jews had been exiled from Rome for a period by Emperor Claudius, and so the Jewish influence had been almost entirely lost to the remaining Gentile church. You can imagine the potential for misunderstanding when the Jewish Christians were allowed to return to Rome. They went back to their spiritual homes to find the scriptures, the rituals, the traditions, and the history of their people largely discounted and forgotten by the Gentile Christians left behind. What a blow that must have been for them. How sad and angry it must have made some of them. And then, when confronted by the returning Jewish Christians, how defensive the Gentile Christians must have been in response.

Paul's letter to the Romans addresses this erupting conflict. From his lifelong immersion in Hebrew scripture, his deep love of God, nurtured through Jewish thought and ritual, he defends and educates his Gentile Christian readers about the continuing validity of Israel in God's purpose and opens his Jewish Christian readers to the depths of God's love through grace and justification by faith.

What a gift to us is our faith ancestors' engagement of all the conflicts in these Christian communities of the first century. Because Paul is willing to wade into this conflict, his most mature and well-reasoned understanding of the nature of God in his letter to the Romans becomes a cornerstone of Christian theology. We are sometimes put off by the anger Paul exhibits in his letters to the Corinthian churches or the churches in Galatia for their quarreling and disagreement. Yet these conflicts become the catalysts that determine the mission of the church, morality, worship, and the nature of the life of prayer.

Paul uses these highly controversial moments in the church to draw his brothers and sisters deeper into the freedom that is theirs in Christ. Conflicts become a means of conversion.

These early congregations invite us to accept the challenge of conflict within the life of our communities. They call us to immerse ourselves in the confusion and vulnerability of disagreement and suggest, in so doing, we will make real the kingdom of God. Look what that conflict can produce, they are saying to us. It can produce a bold church that isn't afraid to let go of a vision of God that is too small or to entertain a greater freedom in Christ that reflects the transforming power of the resurrection. Look what you might leave to the generations to come when you engage with and pray about conflict. It is a powerful means of grace meant to build up the community.

Sometimes I receive a letter from an individual or a group of people who tell me they are leaving their congregation because they disagree with a decision the rector or the vestry has made. No matter how important or seemingly trivial the issue might be, I wonder, as I reflect on the letter, what has been lost to the individual or group leaving, and to the rest in the parish who stay, by not engaging with the contentious issue. I wonder how everyone might have gone deeper in their faith if they had engaged with and prayed about the conflict.

Often on a visitation to a parish, its vestry will tell me how it has sidestepped a potentially ugly confrontation in the parish through compromise with or appeasement of a group or individual member in the church. It is not uncommon for a parishioner to approach me and tell me how hesitant the rector is to deal with conflict or how the ordained leadership prefers to sweep difficult matters under the carpet rather than deal with them in a vestry or congregational meeting. I know it is easy for me to second-guess their decisions, but I can't help but think, given the witness of our ancestors in the faith around conflict, what might have been for these communities if they had faced their disputes.

Sometimes when I pray, I reflect on decisions I have made with committees in the diocese, with parishes, with other religious groups, and with individuals for whom I have been pastorally responsible in the hope of keeping peace. What have I lost by choosing to avoid conflict? What grace have I denied myself or the community that God might have been offering to us? What truth have I been part of denying for the benefit of a future generation of brothers and sisters in Christ?

I ask these questions because it is so clear from Paul's letters and the four Gospels how important communication was to the resolution of conflict. Through letters, debate, meetings held, sometimes at great sacrifice to the participants, the disagreement was engaged. If there is one lesson to be learned from these early church communities around conflict, it is how highly they regarded communication with one another at every possible level.

I heard one evening of a gay couple with two small children who had been attending a church in our diocese. The way I was told the story, this couple had been worshipping with the congregation for about a year, pledging, and volunteering with the other parents in the church nursery when they inquired of one of the ordained members of the staff about the baptism of their youngest son. He said he would get back to them. When the priest did get back to them, the couple was told that because they were gay men in a relationship, the church would not be able to baptize their son.

i went to see the couple in their home the next morning. They told me they had been partners for twelve years, and they had hoped to find a church home for their family in the Episcopal Church. I didn't want the couple to leave the Episcopal Church, so I said we could try a couple of options. I could ask the ordained leadership of the parish if they would be willing to meet with the three of us to discuss the situation, with the hope that they would agree to baptize the boy and continue to include the family in the parish. Or, I said, if they didn't want to subject themselves to potentially painful discussions, I knew another congregation close by that would be more than happy to welcome the two of them and their children.

They chose the first option. Two clergy members, the couple, and I had five meetings together over a period of two months. They were good meetings, hard at times, but honest and, for the most part, respectful and prayerful on the part of everyone. It looked to me as though we had almost reached an agreement on how the parish could baptize the child, honor the commitment of the two men to each other, and still be faithful to the parish's understanding of scripture. It looked like the conflict, because we had engaged with it and prayed about it, had produced a new vision of what the church might be during all the current turmoil over scripture and human sexuality. The rector wanted just one more meeting, this time between the couple and the lay leadership of the parish.

From that meeting, a decision was made by the rector and the lay leadership of the parish that left no option but to end the discussion between the church and the two men and for them to leave the parish. I wonder how much we all lost in that decision. I wonder what would have transpired if the lay leaders of the church had been willing to take a risk and participate in several discussions with the couple, as the clergy had. Because we were unwilling to continue in the conflict, we never had the opportunity to discover what God was asking each of us to sacrifice. I wonder how that parish might have grown by coming to know and love, through all the normal exchanges of Christian community, an openly gay couple and their sons. I wonder if they would have come to know the hospitality of Jesus in a deeper way. And I wonder how the couple might have grown had they been invited to stay. How would they have been transformed through worshipping and serving in a community whose values were so different from their own and yet accepted them? How would I have been changed? What prejudices about conservative evangelical Christians and biblical literalism would I have been forced to let go of?

Painful and as confusing as it might have been for all of us to go on in the discussions and at least try to live together as a church community, I wonder if God wasn't offering all of us, through this conflict between scripture, moral values, and cultures, a greater freedom in Christ. Could God perhaps have been inviting us, without anyone sacrificing deeply held convictions, into a new space where all of us could live as one in Christ? Were we being offered by God in this hard conversation the possibility of a new and resurrected life in Christ?

Talking about What Conflict Means for Your Church

Every three years, in the season of Easter, our lectionary assigns for the Sunday morning gospel the passage from John that includes Jesus saying to Thomas "...I am the way, and the truth, and the life. No one comes to the Father except through me" (John 14:6). That's a puzzling piece of scripture these days. Almost all of us have Muslim and Jewish friends, or people of a different faith with whom we work. We know them to be good and holy people. We have the deepest respect for what they believe. Or, others of us have benefited in our Christian spiritual practices from Buddhist insights or from meditation techniques from other religions. How do we understand, then, that seemingly exclusivist passage from John's Gospel?

The last time that passage came up in the lectionary, I received a number of letters from unhappy individuals in our diocese who had heard sermons that day that questioned the more traditional, exclusive interpretation of John 14:6. The people who wrote to me wanted me to make a clear statement declaring, as they believed the author of John does, that the only way to God is through Jesus Christ. They wanted me to admonish the preachers who challenged this understanding of the passage. We had a conflict on our hands. What would you have done? How would you have responded to the letters? What do you think Paul or Mark would have done with this conflict to strengthen their churches?

Over the years much of the conflict I have witnessed in congregations seems to get focused on the clergy leadership in the parish. The priest might be characterized as not pastoral enough, too authoritarian, not good with details or paying too much attention to details, a poor preacher, or too strident. The reason the ordained person is judged inadequate is always a little different, and sometimes it does have to be acknowledged that the ordained leadership of the parish is inadequate or even abusive. However, my sense from studying conflict in the New Testament communities is that leaders like Paul and Mark always understood a deeper issue worth exploring, an issue underneath the event or person causing the disruption in the community. What do you think? What could be the deeper theological issue underneath a conflict in your congregation? How do you think God might be calling us to build up the community if we engaged with and prayed about this issue? What would we lose if we swept it under the carpet?

Time

"What," I asked the five young people with whom I was having lunch in one of our suburban parishes on a Saturday afternoon, "is hardest about being a teenager?" "All the demands," replied the seventeen-year-old who was sitting to my right. "Yeah," agreed the young woman across from me. She then went on to say, "All the expectations of teachers, coaches, parents, friends, and colleges. There just isn't enough time." I continued my questioning. "So, when did it start to get hard for you?" "When I was ten," answered the youngest teenager at the luncheon. "Why ten?" I asked. "Because," he replied, "at ten you had to choose just one sport. You have to get serious. The competition gets harder, so you only have time for one sport." The other four all nodded in agreement.

"When do you think it gets easier?" I asked. They were quiet for a moment, and then one young man said, "I don't think it does get any easier. I watch my dad. He has to travel a lot. His job is really demanding. He never seems to have enough time." One of the young women added, "It's the same for my mother. She only works part time, but with the four of us at home, the church, and all the other things she does, she never seems to stop." "How about you, Tom?" one of them asked. "What's it like for you?" "Just the same, never enough time," I quietly replied. "I guess," said the daughter of the too-busy mother, "we are all in the same boat."

Time is a big issue for all of us. You talk to me about time frequently. Some of you who are older, especially the women, tell me it isn't like it used to be in the church. You remind me of the days when not many women worked outside of the home. In those days, you say, women had more flexible schedules for meetings and organizing church events. You say that now, with both parents working outside the home, no one has the time to come to meetings, especially those in the middle of the day. You say the hockey, football, soccer, and baseball practices and games of your children and grandchildren take time from away Sunday church attendance and weekend commitments to your parish.

You tell me that a lot of people in your congregations have to work on Saturdays and Sundays. You tell me that time is at such a premium for people that as vestry members and lay leaders, you often hear complaints if Sunday services go over an hour. You tell me there was a lot of resistance from parishioners when you tried to move church school for the children to the hour before worship time and then to introduce adult education. You made this decision so the whole family could participate in Christian education. But people just didn't want to give up that extra hour on Sunday morning.

Sometimes you even take a stab at solving the problem of time. What if, you suggest, we had a service on Saturday night so church wouldn't conflict with sports? Or what if we had more church events professionally catered so we didn't have to spend time with a lot of preparation and cleanup? Could we strictly limit vestry meetings to two hours, you ask, so people might be more willing to volunteer for the vestry? "It's a matter of people sorting out their priorities," someone will often say. "It has to do with time management," another person might add.

With all the responsibilities you have and the demands on your time, when do you have enough time to pray or read the Bible? With your time being at least as valuable as your financial resources, how can you give any more time to your Christian community? What should the balance be in your life between work, family, the church, and the leisure time that God wants you to have? Given your children's interests and the demands in their lives, what expectations should you have of them for worship, youth group, and service? It is clear to me, from the intensity of our conversations, that you know that time for worship is essential to a vibrant relationship with God. You wouldn't give the time you do to your church if you didn't know how critical your time is to building a strong Christian community.

Time, not money or membership, just might be the biggest issue we face today in our personal relationships with God and in our corporate church life. It could be that the problem of time is much bigger than there not being enough hours in the day, the culture in which we live, or the expectations we place on ourselves.

Letting Scripture Talk about Time

What does scripture say to us about time? Did the authors of our Gospels and Paul believe time was an important issue to building strong Christian communities?

Remember how I said in chapter two that there is every reason to believe that the author of the Gospel of Matthew was a teacher? I said that probably he was a kind of Christian version of those Jewish teachers of the late first century who gathered their students around them in places like Sepphoris to teach about the Torah. Because Matthew draws such a vivid picture of Jesus as a teacher of his disciples, you have to wonder if he wasn't, like a good writer of any period in history, writing from his own experience. There are so many occasions in this Gospel where Jesus sends the crowds away or eludes crowds and then, like a teacher of his time, gathers just his disciples in a house or a boat, over a meal, and teaches them. Jesus' desire to have time alone with his disciples may well reflect Matthew's need, as a teacher, to have periods with his students when the crowds were not present (Matthew 9, 10, 11, & 12).

For a few minutes now, use your imagination to recapture the milieu of Matthew that we learned about in chapters two and six. We don't know exactly what is happening in these last decades of the first century in Matthew's part of the world, somewhere in western Syria, but we know from the way he writes that this is a violent and chaotic time. We know, even though it might be now fifteen or

twenty years after the event, that Jews and the Jews who are followers of Jesus Christ are still reeling from the Roman army's destruction of the Temple in Jerusalem in 70 CE. As in almost any war,
villages and towns have been destroyed, people have been displaced,
and life is full of uncertainty and hardship. The tenacity of the Jewish people in the face of Roman oppression has meant some long,
debilitating sieges and cruel and capricious reprisals on the part of
the Roman military.

Memories are long in Middle Eastern culture. An act of generosity between families can bind those families together for generations. A feud between clans can generate hostility between those
clans for decades. The people for whom Matthew wrote his Gospel
around 85 CE would not have forgotten the destruction of the Temple or the horrific suffering of their people at the hands of the
Roman military, even if they hadn't been physically present themselves or even born yet. All of it would have been as real for them as
if it had happened yesterday.

It might have been a conversation among his students, dredg-
ing up just such atrocities inflicted by the Romans on their families
and towns, that prompted some of Matthew's teaching about time.
Imagine it is in the evening and the author of Matthew's Gospel has
these disciples gathered by a fire, sharing their stories. Imagine the
sense of sadness that might have descended on the group as they
remembered the losses they had suffered. As they discussed the many
tragedies that they had endured in the past, it isn't hard to imagine
their fear and anxiety for themselves and their loved ones as they
contemplated the future. It would have been easy for them in a conversation like this to forget about the new life they had been given
by God through Jesus Christ. It would have been very understand-
able, as they talked of the instability of the past, to slip into a discussion of how they could make their lives more secure in the future.

Maybe Matthew has been listening to all of this and, good
teacher that he is, decides this is a teaching opportunity. It is time
for some of Matthew's good, sensible advice. He gets them all seated
and quieted down. Maybe he even offers prayer. He does whatever
he can to give them some space from their fear and anxiety. He

draws together in his mind the sources he has to address in such a situation. Then Matthew begins to speak to his students. This is part of what he has to say to them, using words he remembers from a particular tradition of Jesus that he heard from someone or read in a text that is now lost to us, the Hebrew scripture, and, as a Jewish believer in Jesus of Nazareth, his own understanding of God:

"Therefore, I tell you, do not worry about your life, what you will eat or what you will drink, or about your body, what you will wear. Is not life more than food and the body more than clothing? Look at the birds of the air; they neither sow nor reap nor gather into barns, and yet your heavenly Father feeds them. Are you not of more value than they? And can any of you by worrying add a single hour to your span of life? And why do you worry about clothing? Consider the lilies of the field, how they grow; they neither toil nor spin, yet I tell you, even Solomon in all his glory was not clothed like one of these. But if God so clothes the grass of the field, which is alive today and tomorrow is thrown into the oven, will he not much more clothe you—you of little faith. Therefore do not worry, saying 'What will we eat?' or 'What will we drink?' or 'What will we wear?' For it is the Gentiles who strive for all these things; and indeed your heavenly Father knows that you need all these things. But strive first for the kingdom of God and his righteousness, and all these things will be given to you as well. So do not worry about tomorrow, for tomorrow will bring worries of its own. Today's trouble is enough for today" (Matthew 6:25–34).

Steeped in Judaism, Matthew recalls images and passages from the Hebrew scripture. He uses these passages and images partly because, in this uncertain time, he knows how comforted his students will be by the ancient and familiar. Matthew gives them some perspective on this difficult period by referring back to a time of glory in the life of Israel, the kingship of Solomon (I Kings 10:4–5 and II Chronicles 9:13–22). He reminds them of the transitory nature of human life and the steadiness of God through a passage from the prophet Isaiah (Isaiah 40:6–8). He draws on the wisdom of Judaism by including an offering from Proverbs (Proverbs 27:1). Knowing his community as well as he does and being the good pastor and teacher that he is, Matthew places all these old, familiar passages from the Hebrew scripture in the context of sayings of Jesus that are also known a decade or so later to the author of Luke's Gospel. Matthew adds a few touches of his own to these sayings of Jesus so that they are more easily understood by his students and yet are still faithful to the same source.

It was powerful stuff those scholars heard from their teacher that night, given what they had suffered in the past and whatever fears and anxieties they had about the future. For Matthew is saying that just because Jesus of Nazareth is the fulfillment of God's promise to you doesn't mean that all the trouble in your lives is going to magically disappear. Christ's presence won't make everything suddenly all right for you. But, because Jesus is the Messiah, all time is now God's time. Even this difficult time you are going through now and even what you are afraid of in the future are under the dominion of God. It may not seem like it to you, but you can find God's presence through Christ even now. You no longer have to worry about what is going to happen to you next, because God has shown that God is taking care of you through the suffering, death, and resurrection of Jesus Christ. This time, right now, just as it is, Matthew is saying, is an important opportunity. Look to this time and pay attention to it as part of the unfolding of God's glory.

No wonder someone wrote down what Matthew said that night. No wonder this particular part of the speech was so important for Matthew's students to repeat when they went out to preach and minister in those threatened Jewish Christian communities in western Syria. You can imagine how this knowledge of the assurance of God's dominance and provision would embolden the church. You can understand how, in turn, this knowledge from Matthew's students might have informed the preaching and teaching of the leadership of those house churches and helped them minister to those who were anxious and fearful in their congregations.

How do we hear these ancient words of Matthew in the twenty-first century? How do we become oriented to this teaching of Matthew that understands God's sovereignty over time? How do we open ourselves to this sovereignty of God in all the times of our life?

Prayer is, I think, one way for us to mine this rich vein in the teaching of Matthew on time and let it inform our twenty-first-century conversation on time as we try to build up the communities that God has entrusted to us as they struggle with this issue.

Like many of you, I try to pray and meditate every day. Over the years I have used many traditional forms of Christian meditation, and I have also experimented with adapting Buddhist meditation techniques to my Christian spirituality. While I have been pretty faithful in my prayer for several decades now, I can't say it has ever been the hour of the day to which I most look forward.

You may not have the luxury of a set period of uninterrupted time in which to pray. But all of us have gaps in the day when we can pray: when we are making that daily commute in the car and we resist the temptation to turn on the radio, or when we are standing alone in the shower. Even those few seconds before you have to make a difficult phone call is a time when you can be mindful of the presence of God.

To be honest, not much happens in my prayer. After I have spent some minutes quieting myself and finding a comfortable position in which to pray, my mind is usually full of distractions. As much as I might try to focus on a passage of scripture or some particular image, over and over again I am drawn to thinking about work I have to do that day or problematic relationships, or I just lapse into daydreaming, sexual fantasy, anything but the phrase or passage of scripture I have actually decided to use in my prayer on that day. Occasionally, I experience some deep longing, a sense of joy in my prayer, or I perceive, through some profound feeling I have, that God is calling me to do or not to do some particular thing. But most of the time my prayer is a real battle with distraction and boredom.

While I do try to struggle with this lack of attentiveness in my prayer, I don't let it bother me so much anymore. What I have come to understand over the years is how my meditation time sets me up for the rest of the day. That uneventful hour in the morning seems to open me to all the ways God is breaking into my life and is present in this world throughout the rest of the day. Some words in a meeting, a casual exchange with one of my brothers in the monastery, a difficult pastoral encounter become shot through with the knowledge of God's sovereignty and glory. I never know when an epiphany will happen, but I do know that when I don't pray in the morning, I'm very apt to miss this revelation from God.

My prayer has helped me grasp what Matthew is trying to teach us: there is no such thing as ordinary time. My daily period of prayer seems to draw me away from experiencing time as limited, an enemy that has to be managed or controlled, and opens time to being an experience of the presence of God. My uneventful prayer releases the knowledge within me of possibility and hope, even when my day or, like for Matthew and his students, this time in the world seems hard or overwhelming.

Because through prayer God has opened me to all the ways God might be revealing the self of God to me in the ordinary events of the day, I have been given by God a kind of treasury through which I can anticipate my future. Now a day of loneliness always holds the possibility of falling in love. A long, hard meeting contains the potential for some unimagined breakthrough. A routine worship service or an all-too-familiar piece of scripture may have within it a word I have never heard before. Anxiety, fear, hopelessness, control, and boredom, the enemies of God's experience of time, are sometimes vanquished through the daily discipline of prayer. I am no longer living in a time that is limited or needs to be controlled, but in God's time. This time for Matthew, for you, and for me has been redeemed through Jesus Christ. God is taking care of us now, and God will take care of us in the future as well.

Talking about What Time Means for Your Church

For the most part, the Gospels and Paul seem to have stressed the importance of believers being focused on the fact that God through Jesus Christ has redeemed all time. All time is God's time, and all time will finally be fulfilled in God. Could you have a conversation about how you see this happening in our world today? How do you experience time? Has how you experience time changed over your life? In your prayer, how much do you invite God into decisions you must make about time? Do you think some of our preoccupation with time and our sense of the lack of time might be connected to our avoidance of facing our human limitations and death itself?

It is apparent that our early Christian brothers and sisters spent a great deal of their time communicating with each other. They wrote letters back and forth between churches, they traveled long distances to be with one another, and they organized meetings between churches. Why do you think they were so willing to spend so much time on one another? How do you think they thought their use of time enhanced their commitment to Jesus Christ and built up the body of Christ? Thinking back to our last chapter, on conflict, what is the relationship between the time we spend on communication and conflict?

TEN

Outreach

TO CAPTURE our attention, a newspaper reporter often begins an article with a human interest story. Rather than beginning with sterile facts and figures about how widespread child abuse is, the journalist introduces a particular abused child to us and tells her story. Once the individual story has been told, then the reader has been drawn into the seriousness of the problem and is now ready for more general information.

Letting Scripture Talk about Outreach

Mark's Gospel uses this technique. In chapter five, the writer of this Gospel introduces us to a woman who has been suffering with hemorrhages for twelve years (Mark 5:25–34). She has gone from physician to physician and spent all her money, and yet her condition has grown worse. Immediately, the reader has tremendous sympathy for this woman. She is so obviously alone and destitute, and the reader cannot help but be moved by the hopelessness of her situation. Through the story of this one woman, our attention has been captured, and the author of Mark draws us into the plight of countless women from the Galilee who suffered under the cruelty of the Roman occupation. Women in this part of the world around the time of Jesus, while they were considered the property of their fathers or their husbands, were always cared for by their families, even in sickness and widowhood. The family was the equivalent of our government welfare. But because of the heavy taxation by the Roman government, the puppet governments of men like Herod, and the Temple in Jerusalem, families were being forced from their land and were unable to care for single women and children.

The author of Mark's Gospel wants to draw attention to this terrible situation, and so he writes individual stories, not just of women, but of a whole society of disenfranchised people. He wants to expose the hunger and illness from which people are suffering because there is no food. He wants to show that people like lepers and the mentally ill, who ideally should be cared for, because of the injustice of the government and the Temple, are in fact being abandoned and left to fend for themselves. Jesus, he writes to the little house churches in Antioch, came to change this terrible situation. Jesus came to proclaim a different kind of kingdom: God's kingdom, where women are respected, children cared for, the hungry fed, and the ill healed.

The Jesus of Mark's tradition wanted systemic change. Mark portrays Jesus as a person soaked in the prophetic tradition of Israel and as the initiator or agent of God, bringing God's kingdom into being. Through the death and resurrection of Jesus Christ, the power to continue his work and spread it throughout the world is given to his followers.

All through this Gospel, Mark wants his hearers to know that the disciples of Jesus are meant to participate in the coming of this new kingdom. In imitation of Jesus and his disciples, the members of those small communities in Antioch are meant to see themselves as the disciples of Jesus and therefore as agents of the kingdom of God as well. As early as the Gospel's sixth chapter, his disciples are sent out, on their own, to teach about the kingdom and to heal people.

The author of Mark writes this Gospel to build up these communities in their mission. He wants to show them, through the witness of Jesus and his disciples, not only what God has done for them through Jesus, but what they as followers of Jesus are meant to be doing through their communities. It's like a mission statement for the communities in Antioch. The mission of the followers of Jesus of Nazareth was—and is—to change the system, to speak out against injustice and the status quo, and to provide the healing so desperately needed in the world. In Mark's Gospel, the coming of the new kingdom always means participating in the suffering of the cross.

It is clear in Mark's Gospel that the suffering and death of Jesus are not only inevitable but necessary for the coming of the kingdom of God. Therefore, Mark wants the members of the congregations to whom he is writing to also be clear that if they are joining with Jesus in his work of overthrowing oppression and creating a new kingdom, then they, too, will be required to suffer for this new reality. Systemic change can only happen for the revolutionary Jesus of Mark's Gospel through the cross. So Mark tells the members of his churches in the late 60s or early 70s, and our congregations today, that if you are working for justice, you, too, will be called into the suffering and death of the cross.

Do you see where Mark might be inviting us? Most of us have been part of someone's healing. We have provided casseroles to neighbors recovering from surgery, transportation to critically ill members of our churches for tests, radiation, or chemotherapy treatments. Most of us as well, in one way or another, have gone beyond the immediate scope of people we know and have had the opportunity to offer hope, something of the resurrection, to the disenfranchised. We have served meals in a shelter for the homeless, providing nourishment for people and the knowledge that someone cares about their plight. We have gone on a mission trip or worked locally over a weekend to build adequate housing for a family. We have written checks to alleviate the suffering of an individual or a community affected by some disaster. All of this is a critical witness to the reality of the resurrection.

Mark invites us to a deeper place. He is saying we have strength through the death and resurrection of Jesus Christ to give fullness of life not just to individuals but to whole populations. Mark gives us a sense of the wide-sweeping vision of God through Jesus in the salvation of the world and our role in that vision. He may be speaking most immediately to those house churches in Antioch, but because scripture is a living word, he is saying that our witness as followers of Jesus Christ is meant to change systems that oppress and impoverish whole parts of our society. Here is a recent example of how we have done just that.

In 1998 the Episcopal Church played a critical role in giving literally millions of people around the globe hope for the first time in their lives. We made the resurrection a reality for them. It happened like this. When the Anglican bishops from around the world met at Lambeth in 1998, as they do every ten years, the issue of world debt was on the priority list of almost every one of their provinces.

In an effort to educate bishops of the Episcopal Church for the Lambeth Conference discussions on world debt, Tom Hart and Jere Skipper in the Episcopal Church's Office of Government Relations in Washington, D.C., prepared a paper on the subject. Because of the lack of accessible information on world debt for those without training in economics, the paper proved to be a valuable resource for the Anglican bishops and for a number of Christian denominations and nongovernmental organizations interested in world debt issues.

Following the Lambeth Conference in 1998, our Office of Government Relations led continued work on world debt with three other concerned organizations: Oxfam International, the Catholic Conference of Bishops, and Bread for the World. This group insisted there would be no debt relief globally without the commitment of the United States Congress, so they drafted legislation.

Initially, because they thought there was little chance of the bill passing in a Republican Congress, not even those in the Clinton administration were interested in world debt issues. The road was long and tedious. Doggedly, using the original research for the Lambeth Conference and the drafted legislation, the group set about educating and convincing Democrats and Republicans alike of the importance of this issue. Gradually, they won support from both sides of the congressional aisle. Finally, the bill was signed by President Clinton in an East Room ceremony in the White House on November 6, 2000, after two years of work, which had began with just two staff members of the Episcopal Church's Office of Government Relations.

This was a major victory for the poor and disenfranchised of the world. A system of oppression and injustice was overthrown. Oxfam International, the Catholic Conference of Bishops, Bread for the World, and the Episcopal Church were agents of changing this system, which encouraged human suffering and degradation. If you support any of these organizations or churches, you were involved in changing the lives of millions of people around the globe. For example, if you are a member of the Episcopal Church and offer a pledge to your congregation, a portion of your pledge went to your diocese, which, in turn, sent a portion of your pledge to the national church to fund our Office of Government Relations. Some of us wrote letters to members of Congress, made phone calls, or mobilized people in our congregations to participate in the relief of world debt. The precious financial resources of the poorest countries in the world, which had been serving crippling debt, were now, because of our church, released to provide health services, education, and food assistance for the poor.

What difference did it make? In just one of the forty-one poorest nations in the world, Tanzania, debt relief savings have made it possible for 1.6 million children to receive an elementary school education. More than a thousand new schools were built in the two years following the passage of the legislation in Congress, and almost eighteen thousand new teachers have been recruited. In Tanzania and all across the world, there is new hope and possibility.

In a very real sense, the Episcopal Church, along with the other organizations and churches, in the last decade of the twentieth century, by initiating debt relief for the forty-one poorest nations in the world, embodied Mark's hope for those diverse house churches in Antioch in the 60s CE.

Talking about What Outreach Means for Your Church

It might be a good idea to begin your conversation on outreach by sharing with one another the most satisfying outreach of which you have been a part in your church. Was it going with a group of young people to serve meals to the homeless or working in a food pantry?

Was it working in your church's thrift shop and having the opportunity to hear the stories of the people suffering economically who came in to buy used clothes? Did being that close to someone who had so little in terms of material stability change you? Was it a mission trip to some other part of the country or to another part of the world in which you participated? Were you affected by tutoring a child in an after-school program in an urban congregation?

Did that outreach experience in some way open you to an inequity of our society? For example, through that one child you tutored in reading skills, were you able to see how the large class size of city public schools, the struggling home life of many of our urban children, or the role racism still plays in our country was part of the reason this child wasn't at the appropriate reading level? In spite of your joy at teaching a child to read, or providing food or shelter for a homeless family, did your encounter make you feel overwhelmed by the enormity of some of the problems we face in our country or the world?

Did your experience trouble you enough to make you want to work to change the system that makes it hard for some children to learn or leaves some families without food and housing? Could you talk amongst yourselves as church leaders about what kind of systemic change God might be calling the church to initiate or be part of in your community or state, or in our country? What would your involvement in systemic change look like? How does Mark help you in your response? How would you need to encourage one another? How would you respond to people who say the church shouldn't be involved in systemic change? Are we afraid of disagreeing with one another? Are we afraid we might have to face some part of ourselves that doesn't want to see change? Do you ever give God the opportunity to thank you for the way you have tried to initiate change?

CHAPTER ELEVEN

Evangelism

I T IS ESTIMATED that by the early fourth century, before Christianity was legalized in the Roman Empire, there were already as many as five million Christians living in the countries surrounding the Mediterranean. Extensive road systems and the mobility of people throughout the empire; the fascination in the Roman culture with a new religion with ancient roots in the East; the lack of initiation fees and the classless nature of Christianity; a definite missionary strategy, with a particular focus on urban areas; and, of course, tireless, articulate, powerful figures, like Paul, all contributed to the rapid spread of Christianity. However, as important as all these reasons were to the growth of Christianity, I believe the critical factor in the explosion of membership in the church was the individual witness of ordinary Christians in small house churches across the empire.

Given how similar the presentations of Jesus' teaching can be in the four Gospels, how alike some of the stories of healings and miracles are, and the remarkable congruity in the four accounts of the trial, suffering, and death of Jesus, have you ever noticed how dissimilar the resurrection appearances are in Mark, Matthew, John, and Luke? For example, in Mark there isn't a resurrection appearance, but simply the women finding the empty tomb and the young man dressed in a white robe who tells them that Jesus has been raised from the dead (Mark 16:1–7). Then Matthew offers two stories of Jesus appearing to his disciples. Matthew tells the story of the brief encounter between the risen Christ and the women at the tomb and then Christ's appearance to the eleven disciples on a mountain in the Galilee (Matthew 28:9–20). However, in the Gospel of John, the risen Christ appears to Mary Magdalene in the garden, to the disciples in the room in Jerusalem, and to Thomas, and then Christ comes to the disciples on the beach after they have been fishing, prepares a meal for them, and talks with Peter (John 20 and 21). Finally, Luke recalls two resurrection appearances. He tells the story of Christ revealing his identity at a meal, after he walked with two disciples on the road to Emmaus, and again later, to his disciples in Jerusalem (Luke 24).

It seems the Gospel writers were using these resurrection appearance stories as invitations to the members of their communities to reflect on how Christ was alive for them in Antioch, in Syria, in the northern Galilee, or throughout the Roman Empire in whatever decade they were living. I believe they were trying to get people thinking about how Christ was present to them in their place, in their time.

Letting Scripture Talk about Evangelism

Let me try to explain what I mean through Luke's telling of Christ's appearance to the two disciples in Emmaus. Remember that Luke wrote seventy or eighty years after the death and resurrection of Jesus Christ, and it is likely that some of his congregations included people whose families had been Christians for three or four generations. Could Luke have been thinking of a group of young adult men and women, not recent converts to Christianity, whose parents, grandparents, and perhaps great grandparents had been followers of Jesus Christ?

At the time Luke's Gospel was written, most likely in the early years of the second century, the violence and persecution of the 90s was over, and the Roman Empire had entered a period of relative calm, when there was a fair amount of tolerance toward Christianity. When Luke wrote his Gospel, could he have been addressing a generation of Christian young people who had never experienced a time when Christians were actively persecuted or held in suspicion? This group could not possibly have had the same sense of immediacy about Christ's second coming as their brothers and sisters in Christ to whom Paul wrote some fifty or sixty years before in Thessalonica. Had they, by this time, lost some of the zeal of their ancestors in the faith? Did Luke sense that these young adults were no longer seized by the power of Christ's resurrection in their lives?

Whatever the germ of the Emmaus story was, imagine what it might have been like for one of these ordinary tax-paying people, with jobs and perhaps children, to hear this story told in their church. Wouldn't they have thought:"Of course, that is what it is like for me. So often I don't know Christ is with me, speaking to me, and then later, as I reflect, I know he was there guiding me and teaching me." "Sure," the young, successful cloth merchant, father of three small children, thinks when at the part of the story when the two disciples recognize the risen Christ in the sharing of the meal. "That is what it is like for me. So often it is here in the church, when I am praying and breaking bread with my brothers and sisters, that I feel his presence in my life." Or a young, recently betrothed woman thinks to herself, "Yes, it is often when I am listening to scripture being read that my heart burns within me and I know that Christ is alive."

Through the tradition he received, John also tailored an experience of the resurrection appearances to the needs and experiences of the community to which he was writing. In John, for example, the risen Christ appears to the disciples in the locked house and offers them peace and the forgiveness of sin (John 20: 19 & 23). Remember in what high regard John's churches held friendship, trust, and staying together no matter what. You probably know from your own efforts at living with a group of people how hard that is no matter how well intentioned you all are. There must have been times of deep theological and personal differences. Think what it must have been like for them after some contentious, difficult meeting to worship together, hear scripture read, and, in the breaking of the bread and sharing of the cup, to feel Christ's healing peace and forgiveness moving among them. Surely, you have had that sense in corporate worship of peace and forgiveness in the gathering of the community. How many of the people of John's churches had said to him that when they were all gathered and praying together, they felt peace and forgiveness? Was John trying to communicate to them that when you pray together and feel peace and forgiveness, that is Christ's risen presence in your midst?

Matthew wrote, you remember, as much as fifteen or twenty years before John and Luke did, to churches living in a particularly violent time, with real threats to them from outside of their community. Across the centuries and across cultures, even to our own time, violence and threats often produce the same effect: They have the potential to make us frightened, anxious, and cautious. We can become paralyzed and unable to be decisive and to have any confidence in our authority. If that was indeed the case for the church to which Matthew was writing, you can see why he would want to use the resurrection appearances that had been handed down to him to encourage his people in a more joyful and fearless community, confident of its authority to proclaim the kingdom of God in the life, death, and resurrection of Jesus Christ. In particular, he uses the resurrection appearance to Mary Magdalene and the other Mary to dispel the fear in his troubled community and compel its members in their mission to the world: In Matthew, Jesus tells the two Marys not to be afraid and, instead of clinging to him, to go and tell the brothers in the Galilee (Matthew 28:10).

Since Mark wrote to house churches forming as little as thirty-five or forty years after the resurrection of Christ, is it any wonder that Mark doesn't include any resurrection appearance of the risen Christ to his disciples? These communities, all coming as they did with a different emphasis on who Jesus was for them, had had very little time to reflect on the resurrection and its meaning for them. The event of the resurrection was very new and raw for them. All Mark gave them to ponder and pray over was this story of Mary Magdalene, Mary the mother of James, and Salome going to the tomb to be greeted by a young man, dressed in a white robe, who tells them that Jesus has been raised from the dead and that they are to carry the message to the disciples that the risen Christ will meet them in the Galilee (Mark 16:1–7). As sparse as Mark's Gospel is concerning the resurrection, he wants to build up his communities by letting them know that fear is not the end of the story of Jesus of Nazareth, who suffered and died. As Luke's, John's, and Matthew's churches would have had the opportunity to do for decades after them, he seems to be inviting his communities to pray and reflect on the mystery of the resurrection. He wants his people to engage with this profound event in their community's life.

Why did all four Gospel writers invite the members of their congregations to reflect on the reality of Christ's risen presence in their lives? Read now how each one ends his Gospel:

"So they went out and fled from the tomb, for terror and amazement had seized them, and they said nothing to anyone, for they were afraid" (Mark 16:8).

"And Jesus came and said to them, 'All authority in heaven and on earth has been given to me. Go therefore and make disciples of all nations, baptizing them in the name of the Father and of the Son and of the Holy Spirit, and teaching them to obey everything that I have commanded you. And remember, I am with you always, to the end of the age'" (Matthew 28:18–20).

"Now Jesus did many other signs in the presence of his disciples, which are not written in this book. But these are written so that you may come to believe that Jesus is the Messiah, the Son of God, and that through believing you may have life in his name" (John 20:30–31).

"Then he opened their minds to understand the scriptures, and he said to them, 'Thus it is written that the Messiah is to suffer and to rise from the dead on the third day, and that repentance and forgiveness of sins is to be proclaimed in his name to all nations, beginning from Jerusalem'" (Luke 24:45–47).

These quotations are the final words Mark wrote to his forming house churches in Antioch in the late 60s or early 70s CE, that Matthew wrote to his community in western Syria around 85 CE, that John wrote to his congregations in the northern Galilee and southern Syria at the end of the first and the beginning of the second century, and that Luke wrote maybe a few years after John to the churches across the whole Roman Empire. Written across the span of forty or fifty years, these were words for very different communities, with their own internal and external struggles, their own particular experiences of Jesus of Nazareth, and, most likely, their individual ways of worshipping God through Jesus Christ. The membership of some of these congregations was largely Gentile, others were mostly Jewish, and some were a mixture of both, and it appears that more than a few of these communities were perhaps uncertain of the person of Jesus of Nazareth. Yet these writers end their Gospels with the same message. Mark, Matthew, John, and Luke all wanted the people of their communities to spread the good news that Christ is alive and is Lord, and that the kingdom of God had come in Jesus Christ. They knew these followers of Jesus would be most convincing to the people they encountered if they had fully appropriated Christ's risen presence in their own lives.

Even Mark, who doesn't speak directly of proclamation, encouraged his people to tell the story. Himself a consummate teller of stories, who tells more of them than any of the other Gospel writers, Mark knows that stories spread good news. He knew that in telling the stories of all that Jesus had done and ending with one about the mysterious man in the white robe, his people couldn't help but go forth into the world, proclaiming the good news. Mark's plan of evangelism was simply for his people to go forth and tell the stories.

Twenty centuries later, the resurrection appearances in the four Gospels are meant to stimulate the members of our congregations to articulate how we experience the risen Christ in our lives. This is how I respond to Luke's invitation, or that of Mark, John, or Matthew, to explore my own experience of Christ's risen presence in my life. How do I know Christ is alive?

Sometimes in my vocation as bishop when I meet with adults who are being received into the Episcopal Church, I tell them how much I love being the one who officially invites them into the Episcopal Church. It isn't just because I want our congregations to grow in numbers. It is something much more personal for me. I love being part of extending a welcome to new members in the church because, as I have prayed and reflected on my journey with God, it is through the community of the church that I have experienced the risen Christ and become certain that he is alive, now.

I am a little like those two disciples walking with Christ on the road to Emmaus. Like them, I haven't always known that it was Christ accompanying me on this journey that I began with God through Christ in baptism all those years ago. It is only now, decades later, that my heart sometimes burns within me for all the ways that Christ has been alive for me in the people of the community of the church. How two long-ago Sunday school teachers and an acolyte master drew a difficult, insecure boy into his dignity as a human being. How an eccentric, not very able seminary professor opened a young man to prayer and a personal relationship with God. How scripture and the weekly sharing of the meal with brothers and sisters have consistently invited me into the pattern of Christ's dying and rising and then supported me, making real for me the freedom in Christ that Paul has promised us.

For what was the pattern of his life? It was to confront everything in his world that imprisoned people, all that made them live in small suffering places. He set out to defeat the systems, and the men who represented those systems, that were starving widows, driving people into poverty, causing children to be abandoned, and keeping people from knowing God's abiding love for them. He wanted to make people free. This is the reason he died. The men who supported those systems were threatened by Jesus, and they killed him. But God raises Jesus from the dead and through him initiates a new kingdom, a new system, which makes it possible for all of us to move from cramped places of suffering to the wide-open space where freedom reigns.

Through baptism, the church invited me into the pattern of Jesus, making it possible for me to die to the systems within me that imprison me and then to raise me to new life. Through baptism, the church invited me not only into my own freedom, but to join God through Jesus Christ in the liberation of all people in the kingdom of God initiated in Jesus' life, suffering, death, and resurrection.

He is alive for me in the body of Christ, the church. I am aware of his risen presence, like the two disciples on the road to Emmaus, not every second of every day, but in flashes, and enough to give me hope for myself and for the whole world. This is why I love to welcome men and women into the life of the church. I know they, too, through Christ's risen presence in the church, can know that they and the whole world are being saved. This is why the writers of the Gospels send us out to tell our story, our good news, so others, so the whole world, might participate in the coming of the kingdom.

Talking about What Evangelism Means
for Your Church

Let's begin this question section a little differently this time. Now that you have finished this chapter, before you go on to discuss the questions with the rest of your group, just think for a few minutes about all the people you know in your church. Who would you say appears to be most conscious of Christ's risen presence in his or her life? What makes you choose this person? Have you ever heard this person speak of how he or she knows Christ is alive and active in the world? Do you have any idea if this person ever speaks to others about Christ's living presence in his or her life?

Now turn to yourself. What do the Gospel writers elicit from you concerning your experience of Christ's living presence? In what way did the Emmaus story get you thinking of how he is alive for you? Sometimes people tell me that at the time of communion, they are overcome with a sense of peace; how do you connect that with the appearance of the risen Christ to the disciples in John 20? Or when have you known Christ's presence in the forgiveness of sin or in the act of forgiving another, the way the disciples do in John 20? How have you in your life lived out the demand of the Gospel writers to go out and tell the good news in Christ? Under what circumstances have you told another person of your experience of the risen Christ? Was that awkward for you? Do you have any sense of what your witness meant to them? How did you know it was the right time to speak to them? Do you ever pray about how you are called to be an evangelist?

How do you think your congregation communicates to others the reality of the risen presence of Christ? When do they do it well and with confidence? How do you think the members of your church understand evangelism and these passages that end each of the Gospels? How could you as spiritual leaders of your community help them to articulate this message? How do you as the spiritual leaders of your congregation usually discuss your role concerning evangelism?

Epilogue

THE LONGER I reflect on these early church communities for whom scripture was written, the more aware I am of the ordinariness of these men and women who gathered in these forming congregations. The people in these little congregations to whom Paul, Mark, Matthew, John, and Luke wrote met mostly in homes and were not professional theologians. They had no ordained leadership to definitively settle disputes. It looks like they were sailing in pretty uncharted waters most of the time.

There is no doubt they argued with one another a good deal, that they often got it wrong, and that they were very much people of their time and place. Yet it also looks to me like the writers of the four Gospels and Paul had tremendous respect for these faithful followers of Jesus. Even when Paul was so angry with the people of a particular congregation, it is clear that he, like the writers of the four Gospels, believed that as ordinary as these men and women might be, they were worthy to be the bearers of the good news. They crafted their letters and their Gospels for these communities because they thought they were worth it. They considered the recipients of their writings worth it not because the writers felt these men and women were the best qualified owing to the depth of their faith, material resources, or intellectual gifts, but because of their willingness to engage the risen person of Jesus Christ through worshipping and living together in these small communities.

With their keen awareness of their church communities apparent in the way that Paul, Mark, Matthew, John, and even Luke each use the stories and teaching of Jesus, you could say the writers of the Gospel and Paul were writing scripture with the ordinary people of their congregations. For much of the material in each of the Gospels and the letters so clearly reflects debates, concerns, and struggles in the life of particular communities. Together, they were creating God's word.

Engagement with one another through the life, death, and resurrection of Jesus Christ as it was handed down to them was critical in the building up of these small forming communities. I think Paul, Mark, Matthew, John, and Luke ask the same of us today. I think they want you to be engaged through conversation with others and with scripture in order to build up the life of your church. I believe our ancestors in the faith would have as much trust in you as they did in the ordinary people to whom they wrote their letters and Gospels. The witness of their writings says that you are critical to the continuing revelation of God's word.

About the Author

M. Thomas Shaw, SSJE, is the bishop of the Episcopal Diocese of Massachusetts, and has been a member of the Society of St. John the Evangelist for the past thirty-two years. He has written numerous articles for *Episcopal Life* and the *Episcopal Times* and is a contributing author of the book *How Long O Lord.*